MOTHERHOOD

Am I Doing This Right?

ISBN: Paperback: 978-1-7323579-2-1

First Edition, May 2020

Published by:
Hidden Hollows Publishing
HiddenHollows.net
1306 Blanchard Ave
Flint mi 48503

Printed in the United States of America

This is for my husband who supports me,
my kids who always love me,
my dad and my nephew who changed me and taught me.

DISCLAIMER

I would like to start this book off with a disclaimer for you to keep in the back of your mind as you read it. It is two fold.

1. I love my children more than I ever thought possible. There have been times when I didn't think I could possibly enjoy them and they brought me anxiety. Those days are over and I have a deep love for them that I can't even put into words. Sometimes they drive me B-A-N-A-N-A-S. But sometimes I drive them crazy, too. So please keep that in mind. And let that give you hope if you are in the thick of it with your kids. It is possible and probable you will soon love them more than you ever dreamed.

2. I actually do not hate the medical field. I have many many close friends who are medical professionals and respect and love them. I have had multiple interactions with my kids and my own medical providers that were respectful and productive and wonderful. But I have also had multiple experiences that I walked away feeling the opposite. Those taught me a lot. Those are more interesting than the mundane and not included in this book. But keep in mind I don't hate or shun modern medicine.

Ok that should be everything. I hope you enjoy the stories you are about to read!

CONTENTS

Chapter 1

BEFORE BABIES

I have always wanted to be a mom. Always. Well, at least for as long as I can remember. Is this because I always hated being told what to do and wanted to be the one doing the telling? Maybe. But that's beside the point. The point is, more than being a wife, my heart has always longed to be a mom. Really, I think at some point finding a husband was just a stepping stone to becoming a mom. I did dream about my wedding and my future husband as many girls do, but before that, I dreamt of having little babies.

I remember playing with baby dolls as a kid and pretending that those babies were my babies. Not my friend the baby doll or just "a baby" but my literal offspring that I was charged to take care of and nurture. I was like a dog who attached itself to a toy and truly believed the toy was its own flesh and blood. (Did your dog ever do that? My dog got super attached to some type of toy and got very protective of it. She even started producing milk. It was weird.) Anyway, I would go through the American Girl catalog and drool over the Bitty Baby section. I wanted all of it. The crib, the high chair, the car seat, everything. My child needed it. What else was an 8-year-old mother to do? Pretend that I had these things? Never. Could you pretend your newborn had a highchair or car seat? I never got most or any of it, but I sure spent hours thinking about it all. There are countless pictures of me as a little girl, starting at maybe age 2 or a little younger cradling baby dolls. Holding them and singing, holding them and playing, taking care of them. There is even a home video of me sitting at the kitchen table singing an original song about how someone had broken into my house and broken something that belonged to my kids. I remember the words to this day. "How could they break itttt? How could they break ittt?" Alright, so those are the only words I remember. I know for sure I looked up and saw my dad doing the dad stance with a camcorder recording me. (For my younger readers, a camcorder is a device that took really large...memory cards...and recorded video. It was about as big as a grown man's head and was not a part of your phone. Those were attached to the wall.)

One Christmas I opened the motherload. It was the biggest box that I had ever seen and inside was dozens and dozens of outfits for my daughter. My doll. My pretend babydoll. Outfits and a diaper bag, bottles - one with juice, one with milk. A bassinet and diapers. I had it all. I could finally give my baby girl the life she deserved.

As I got older and played with my American Girl dolls, my daughter Kit and I would go on harrowing journeys together. We were always running away from something or someone. She had her own room in my room. I had a bed and closet for her set up next to mine. At any given time something would happen and I would pack a bag of her clothes and mine. I would bundle her up and we would take the long walk to my closet. Inside it would be dark, cold, drafty even, but I would have a flashlight so we could see each other. I would always look her in her little doll eyes and assure her I would keep her safe. Wow, typing that and seeing it in black and white makes me realize what a weirdo I was. I wonder, if my mom had known about the games I was playing, if she would have had me committed. Or at least taken my children.

My parents did know that I wanted to be a mom. My mom remembers me talking about wanting at least five kids. I had names for them and I apparently talked about them enough for her to commit that to memory. I remember watching my mom and wanting to be a mom like her. She had her flaws and made her fair share of mistakes, but she always knew what to make for dinner. No matter what day of the week or what we had going on, she could always pull a meal together in no time. I still can't remember to stock the basics in my kitchen like flour and breadcrumbs. Above that, my mom always knew what to say when I was scared or anxious. Even if she did not know how to make it better, I always felt like I could go to my mom and she would provide a way out and help me figure out how to make it better. Maybe this was why I always was able to guide Kit through the trenches and away from kidnappers - I had such a strong role model. My dad was an incredible man as well. He worked long hours but I don't remember him not being around. He was there. He was there to listen to me when I had issues. He was funny. He was THE funny guy. Everyone wanted to be my dad's friend. And I got to be his daughter. That is like a badge of honor that I wish I had recognized back then. When I was growing up my dad was quick to tell us if we had done something to disappoint him but also when he was proud of us. I remember my 16th birthday, my dad had a dozen pink roses sent to me in school. I still have two of those roses. I was so excited when they got delivered to me with a sweet note. I wish his pride in me would have given me the confidence to see that I did not need some guy in high school to notice me. But it didn't. Some, sure. But not as much as it SHOULD have.

As I grew even older and the childish things were put away, it was not acceptable to play with American Girl dolls anymore; I had a new mission. I needed to find a man to father my children. I wanted less to be a mom and more to be a girlfriend. To be wanted, to be loved. Then we would have our five children. I thought that meeting someone and falling in love in high school was perfectly reasonable. By my calculations I could graduate at 18, get married that summer and still have a year of marriage under my belt before I became a mother at the age of 19. There were, however, a few things working against me. No boys liked me in high school. I was weird and unpopular. When I was in high school I was a cheerleader and on the dance team. Perhaps that sounds like a good thing but I assure you it was not. Not at my high school. We were not very good dancers nor were we very good cheerleaders. I have many memories of people standing outside of our practices and mocking us.

I was an awkward, insecure, gangly girl who just wanted to have BABIES. I was not allowed to date in high school. My parents thought I was too young and could get into too much trouble. I resented them for it; they were standing in the way of my dreams. My future. I grew rebellious and moody. Eventually after enough sulking my parents started to get worn down. So after some conversations and begging, I was allowed to date. I really thought the lines were going to start forming after the decree was lifted. "Please, boys, one at a time," I'd casually say. ...I had one boyfriend in my entire high school experience. One. We dated from Thanksgiving to just after Valentine's Day my junior year. By "dated," I mean I was his girlfriend on MYSPACE. MY. SPACE. Am I really this old? If a 16-year-old reads this, are they even going to know what in heaven's name I am talking about? I don't think so.

But my boyfriend and I never kissed. Nor did we hold hands. I think we hugged a few times. We talked on the phone. AOL Instant Messengered a lot. We hung out in groups. It was pretty boring. I broke up with him because he said on Myspace he thought he had found the woman who would be his wife. And I DEFINITELY had a crush on another guy at school. So I called him and broke up with him. My mom sat with me when I called him and broke up with him. It was really hard, and he did not see it coming. I felt really bad because I had really hurt him. My mom cried with me. She told me it hurt her to see me in so much pain. But (*bonus*) that boy that I had a crush on saw me crying at school and asked if I was ok. So I guess you could say it was all totally worth it.

I would like to tell you that this all changed for me when I hit college. I really found myself and I was, like, popular or something. This would be false information. Am I painting a clear enough picture for you? I wasn't hideous. Kids did not point at me and then run away. I had a nice face. I was in my early 20s and I still never knew how to use a round brush. I had, well still have, blonde hair that fell flat and was never styled properly. I worked as a receptionist at a hair salon and the stylists were not shy about telling me how I was messing up my hair. I had done my make-up the exact same way every day since I was able to wear make-up at the ripe age of 13. Sure, my eyeshadow color changed from blue to white to brown. Or whatever color it was that I smashed into the creases of my eyelids. I fumbled my way through multiple schools and degree programs trying to figure out what I wanted to do or to be. I did not date. I wanted to date. I wanted a boyfriend. I wanted a wedding. I wanted to have sex. I wanted to be pregnant. I wanted to have a baby. I wanted to be a stay-at-home mom. But there is not a degree for that.

I spent two years of my life living in Texas and trying to figure out who I was. In some ways it worked and I learned a lot. I made a lot of great friends. But I also never really grew into the secure person I needed to be. I was interested in many a man down there. And not a man was interested in me. Seemed like the brunettes were having men fall for them left and right. So I dyed my hair dark brown. I was still desperate and chasing after people I had no business chasing after. I was known as the girl with "a plan but no man." Which was the problem; I was chasing a dream I had. I was not trying to figure out who I was and let life happen to me. So it was let down after let down. I needed to let a guy chase me. It hurt and it was difficult and I have a fair share of regrets from that time. But man, I look back and I think I am grateful. Grateful that I was not in a meaningless relationship when I sat down in a college class in the fall of 2011.

Chapter 2

LOVE STORY

In the fall of 2011, I sat down on the first day of my first college class after I had taken almost 2 years off. I sat down and I saw a kid that I knew because of Facebook. We had gone to the same high school but he transferred to the school for his junior year, the year after I had graduated. We had several mutual friends, and I immediately texted my friend and my sister and said, "That Phil kid from OCS is in my class. But I am not going to talk to him!"

So naturally, 2 days later I turned to him and said, "You went to OCS, right?" Later that day he friended me on Facebook and Skype. We started talking, and I realized we had a lot in common. He wanted to work at his church when he finished college, we liked the same music and books. We had a lot to talk about, and I quickly found that I enjoyed talking to him.

After that conversation, it was infatuation for him. He was 2 years and 2 months younger than me and instantly off my list of possibilities. Because, remember my friends, I wanted BABIES, so a younger man is not going to want to settle down. Plus, with all my confidence and popularity surely there was someone in my age bracket that I would fall for. At some near-future time.

When it was time to study for our first test of the semester I asked him if he could meet me at the library to study. He was super smart and made studying easier. We both got As on that first test. We talked nearly every day and hung out after class around campus. Sometimes he would try and ask me to do things not school-related and I would say no. I did not want him to get the wrong idea. Oh little boy, we will never be more than just friends. He tried to talk to me about "us" or what we were. But I always changed the subject. I made it very well known that I was talking to other guys at the same time. Which I sorta was, but nothing really serious. It was just desperate Mary trying to find a man my age to settle down with.

He slowly got me to hang out for non-school-related things. We agreed to go to a movie, but I quickly tried to bail. He would not take no for an answer and came and picked me up. I texted my mom, "I think I am going on a date." The movie was fun; he paid for me. It was a sad movie, but I enjoyed being with him. He started to become my favorite person to be around. He was kind, funny, he listened, he thought I was hilarious, he was honest, he was...cute. You see, Philip had everything I could ever have imagined in a husband. He is tall (6'1"); had I chosen to wear heels around him, he still would have been taller than me. He had a smile that put me at ease whenever I saw him. He had swooping blonde hair and the most beautiful blue eyes. The kind of eyes that my daughter Kit had had in my childhood. Only they were real and they would look significantly less creepy on a child than Kit's. I did not let myself dwell on those thoughts. Not for long anyway.

I happened to be near his parent's house one night, and I went over to hang out with him. I walked into the house, and his little brother said, "So you're the girl he's been talking about." It was awkward, but I brushed it off. I had known, of course, he was into me. I was an older woman. I had tattoos. I was a catch..well, that is how he made me feel. "Poor kid," I thought to myself. "Will I break his heart?"

I met his parents; his mom got me a bowl of ice cream. We went downstairs and watched Law & Order: SVU. A show he did not care about but I was really into. We sat in two armchairs instead of the couch. I could not have him try and cuddle with me! When he walked me to my car I stuck out my arm as far away from my body as I could get and started implementing a secret handshake which we had never rehearsed. Couldn't have him try and kiss me! I got in my car and thought, "I could see myself hanging out with them a lot;" and the walls I had put up began to crumble even more.

Just a few days later, I woke up in the middle of the night, I sat straight up in bed and said, "I like Philip." I could not deny it anymore. A couple of days later, we had plans to go to the mall, shopping for his birthday. Our class got out early and we went to Starbucks. I sat down next to him and blurted out, "So that thing that you keep wanting to talk to me about...we can talk about it." "Oh..well, I like you," He said. "I like you, too." I don't remember the rest of that cup of coffee, but I know we walked out being boyfriend and girlfriend. I got in his Jeep and we drove to the mall to go shopping, and regret washed over me.

Boyfriend? Girlfriend? Am I sure? Do I even really like him enough to take myself off of the market? No, I don't. I rushed into this. I spent that night calculating in my head how long would be a respectable amount of time I could date him before I broke up with him. He was still my favorite person to talk to and be around, so we hung out and talked for a week. Nothing really changed. About 10 days into our relationship, our parents wanted to meet. So the six of us went out to dinner, then back to my parents' house. It felt natural, it felt right. I relaxed into being his girlfriend a bit more. When it was time for him to leave, I walked him out to his car. His parents had gone home earlier in the evening. We stood in my dark driveway and I let him hug me. He asked if he could kiss me and I said yes. The moment we kissed - listen, I don't care how cheesy or ridiculous this sounds - when he kissed me, my head started spinning and my whole body filled with butterflies. I felt like I was floating and there were fireworks shooting off all around me. I had kissed a few guys before, but I had never in all of my life felt something like that. I know it is super cheesy but I don't care, it is the TRUF! I went inside and told my mom and my sister that he had kissed me. I was giddy. I think

I might have been in love.

He went away on a family trip about a week later, and I went shopping with my mom and sister and I started looking at engagement rings. In early January, I was at his house and it was late at night and I was trying not to fall asleep. He woke me up and said, "Are you sleeping?" Annoyed that he wouldn't let me rest I said, "No, why?" He said, "Because I love you." I said I loved him too.

After we exchanged "I love yous" we started talking about a future together. I knew I wanted to marry him and he knew he wanted to marry me. It was just a matter of time. We used to go to a restaurant and order a dessert to share and read the book 101 Things To Know Before You Get Engaged. Every question we asked each other just reaffirmed that he was the one for me. We had extremely similar ideas and if they differed, we could explain our side and the other person would agree that it made sense to do it another way. One night we talked about baby names. I told him if we...I ...if I ever...have a girl I want the name to be either Molly, Maizie, or Lorelai. He said Maizie sounded like a horse, Lorelai was clearly from a TV show and therefore out, and he liked Molly. So, Molly it was.

On our six month dating anniversary, I drew him a picture of the ring I wanted when we got engaged. I did not know it, but he kept that picture in his wallet and a few months later he would sell his Jeep and get that exact ring made for me. This man is unreal.

In February of 2012, my dad started to feel a bit off. He went to doctor after doctor and they all told him he was imagining things. One evening my brother called me and told me to meet him and his wife, Laura, so they could talk to me. I called Philip on the way and told him I was really worried that something was wrong. He assured me it was probably nothing. When I walked into the kitchen, Adam and Laura were sitting at the kitchen table. I was standing in the doorway, and he said the words that I will never forget.

Love Story

"Dad has a brain tumor." The room spun, but not in a good way. I felt dizzy, disoriented, shocked. I had a lot of questions and there weren't a lot of answers. A short time later my dad had brain surgery to remove the tumor and test it for cancer. Philip came to the hospital with me. He sat with me for the entire surgery. When it was over, the surgeon called us behind a screen to talk with us. He said they had biopsied the tumor and that it was cancer. Cancer. I looked to my brother who had become the patriarch of the family at that moment, and I watched the color drain from his face. No. No. This was not good. I could not take it. I ran away. I ran to the drinking fountain and Philip followed closely behind. He found me and wrapped his arms around me, and I buried my face into his chest and sobbed. "I can't do this," I said. I can't have a parent with cancer. I don't know how to do this. He told me he didn't know how to do this either, but he would be with me. This man who could have left in that moment. He was not tied to me, we weren't even engaged. But he chose to stay and be my anchor through it.

My dad got diagnosed with a glioblastoma, grade 4. They say it is the most aggressive form of brain cancer. If you know someone close to you who has ever gotten a cancer diagnosis, you know that it is terrible. I would not wish that on anyone. I had to carry on with my normal life and do mundane things like go to class. I would sit in class unable to see the notes I was taking because my eyes were always filled with tears. Around me people would argue with the professor about a grade, classmates would be gossiping about other people. It made me mad. Didn't they get it? My dad was fighting for his life. None of this other crap mattered. But still I went on with life. I would go to work or class then go home and spend some time talking with my dad. We all had hope and for a while, it looked like he was beating it. But in June of 2012, he had a follow-up appointment and the tumor was back. In just a couple of months, my dad declined. It was hard to see someone you look up to get so weak and so frail. Philip was my escape. If I could not be in my house anymore, I went to his house. Even before all of this, he was my best friend. I always wanted to be around him, especially when I was upset.

Love Story

In late July I went with Philip's family on a vacation to Florida. While we were there Philip took me on a fancy date. We got really dressed up and went to dinner. We walked around the city and people stopped us and told us we were a really cool looking couple. We walked around a marina and I tried to see if there was a ring box in his pocket. I never saw one so I was a little annoyed that he was setting me up to think he was proposing. We turned a corner and on the ground was an ice bucket, a candle, and two glasses. "THIS IS IT!" I thought. I sat down, and Philip started digging through the ice bucket and pulled out a ring box. He opened it and I saw the most sparkling ring I have ever seen. He told me he loved me and asked me to marry him. I said "YES!" I put the ring on my finger and we were engaged. I called home to tell my family the good news. That night I just stared at my beautiful ring; it was exactly what I wanted and it meant I was going to be PHILIP'S WIFE. I would imagine that everyone that knew Philip and his brother wanted to be a Piasecki Girl - but I was going to be one. I WON!

For the rest of our trip, we started making wedding plans. I started crafting my perfect future with my perfect man. We got home and I could not wait to talk to my dad. But he asked me to stop talking to him about the wedding. He said it made him too sad. I had hoped that my dad would still be at my wedding, that he would pull through this. I could not imagine my life without my dad. I couldn't imagine a wedding without my dad walking me down the aisle. I couldn't and I wouldn't. Until I had to. Hospice came and told us they did not think he would make it through the weekend. I went down to where my dad laid in my living room in a hospital bed. I kissed him on the head and the corner of his mouth turned up in a smirk, but he did not open his eyes. I went upstairs and laid in my bed and wanted it to all go away.

A few hours later... He was gone. It felt so final. There was nothing else we could do to try and keep him here. It was done. He had put up a good fight and it was time for him to rest.

Love Story

At the funeral, I gave a eulogy for my dad. I was so nervous to speak in front of people that I never let myself cry. In fact, I comforted people who came to me crying about my father's death. My dad was well-loved. He was an incredible man. One of his best friends spoke at the funeral. My dad had told him he knew he was dying but he didn't want us to know. My dad was a painter and he told his friend if he had the chance, he would like to paint each one of his kids one last painting. For me, he would have painted a bride. My whole body shook with sobs after I heard that.

After the funeral, I threw all of my energy into wedding planning even though there was a huge dad-shaped hole in my heart. I had crafted this idea of what my life would look like when I grew up. Of course in my mind my future was going to be wonderful. I had designed it perfectly with the perfect man at the perfect wedding, then we would have the perfect kids and live the perfect life. I had thought about it so much, it was almost tangible. But when the doctor told us my dad had cancer, a huge crack formed in it. And when he died, the entire thing shattered in my hands. During our engagement over the next 10 months, I slowly picked up each piece and dreamed of a new future. This future was different than I'd imagined before - not worse or better, but different.

I wonder if you're still reading this. I wonder if I have completely lost your attention because you maybe got this book because you're a mom and wanted to read about motherhood. This book is my story to and through becoming a mom. Meeting my husband and baby daddy, losing my dad, and as you'll find out, another very important person in my life - that's all part of it. Everything I am going to be sharing with you has shaped me into the mom I am today. As I am writing this my six-month-old son is rolling around on the ground. I never thought I would get here. I thought I would be grieving my dad's death for the rest of my life. But I am on the other side of it. I am a mom, I have that experience in my head and heart, but I am able to breathe again. Being raised by Tom Hallett and losing Tom Hallett has shaped my motherhood and my marriage. Some good things, like truly not sweating the small stuff, but also it brought up a lot of anxiety. When I thought of the worst-case scenario that day and it came true, it became a lot harder to convince me that worst-case scenarios wouldn't always happen.

Philip and I got married on June 14th, 2013. We had planned the wedding through my deep grief, but we had put together a beautiful wedding. On the afternoon of the wedding, I got ready with my bridal party and my mom. I was excited. It was sad knowing my dad was not there, but it was a beautiful day and I was about to be Mrs. Piasecki. Our wedding was down at Philip's parents' lake and there were no clouds in the sky that day. As an acoustic version of "I Need A Hero" played, I walked down the aisle with my mom and my big brother on either side of me. I looked down and saw my groom standing there. He looked as hot as ever and I could not wait to be his. So I could kiss him whenever I wanted. He had shaved his head, and I couldn't help but think how much older and more mature he looked standing there. We had been through so much together and I was ready to take on our perfect future together. We promised to love each other forever, to take care of each other and to lead each other to Christ. I don't remember all that was said, but I do remember Pastor Ernesto pronouncing us man and wife. It was perfect.

After that, we went on to our reception. It was without a doubt one of the best weddings I have ever been to. We ate good food and danced. It was a party and it was incredible.

So, in case you're reading this and you're not a married person. Or not a young adult. Or maybe just have never experienced this. But there is a phenomenon that happens as soon as you are married. Sometimes even at your very wedding. People came up to us at the reception and started asking when we were going to start having kids. It annoyed me in some ways. It seemed a bit intrusive. Like, why are you asking me when I am

Love Story

going to start having unprotected sex, friend of my mother? So, despite the intrusive smalltalk, we finished the best party in history, and got to start on the rest of our lives together.

Chapter 3

DESIGNING THE DREAM

Starting during our honeymoon and for the next several months, that was the only time in my memory I did not want to be a mom... at that moment. It was always in the back of my mind, but I wanted some time to be Philip's wife. We tried very hard not to become pregnant. But that all quickly faded. We moved from an apartment into our current house; I think that is when baby fever spiked real hard. So that's when I started asking Philip when HE wanted to start having babies. I had to at least get him thinking about it. Let's be real; I am sure he saw right through what I was trying to do. I picked out the paint color for the "spare room" with a nursery in mind. Philip was painting the "spare room" and looked up at me and said, "Wait. This...is a nursery color!!" And I smiled and said, "Well..we won't have to repaint it when it IS a nursery." Really I was doing HIM a favor. He should have thanked me.

While I was out grocery shopping a couple of times I bought a few pieces of baby clothes. I couldn't help it. They called out to me! Then they were suddenly in my buggy! They were little and they were cute and they were going to be mine. I hid them in the back of my closet so Philip would not know how crazy I was. Really, I was buying a few items here and there so it would not be as expensive later. I was doing HIM a favor. He should have thanked me.

I began to ask Philip if he was sure we wanted to wait two years to have babies. Two years from now? Or like two years from when we got married? Or... two years from when we got engaged? How committed to this "two year" thing are you? Don't we want to be young parents? If we started now, we could be done having kids by the time you're 30. If we start trying now it could take us 2 or 3...even 8 months to get pregnant!

This is when I started to read and 'pin' mommy blogs for hours. Philip and I would sit on the couch in our basement and watch movies or he would play a video game and I would pin the pins. I became an Expert Pinterest Mom. Carefully crafting my motherhood techniques before ever even having a baby implant itself in my uterine wall. I went over nursery decor, labor strategies, baby names, baby clothes, and child-rearing. Anything mom-related, I wanted to know all about it.

I would ask Philip constantly things like, "When we have kids we won't let them watch a lot of TV... right??" "Of course not," he would respond. Of course not. We were not lazy people and we would not have lazy TV-watching kids. No, our kids would have sensory bins and mountains of books to look at. They would have just a few minimalistic and educational toys that would keep them occupied all day. All of these toys would be made from natural organic grass-fed free-range wood. Only the best for our kids.

Some questions were a bit more complex than others. I would ask him something and if he would say the wrong thing, I would give him a shocked look and he would change his answer. He learned very quickly to respond to my questions appropriately so I would not have to go into a lecture on why his response was not the one I was looking for. For some odd reason, he hadn't spent hours upon hours thinking about all the intricacies of parenting our potential children. Go figure.

Designing the Dream

I don't understand why he did not want to know the exact swaddling method that could ensure our baby would sleep. Our baby would not only sleep but, as I learned in my research, sleep regressions are actually myths. If you train your baby when its nights and days are, then they will sleep through the night very early on. They would learn how to soothe themselves in any dark room with a sound machine and they would not stray from it. All babies really actually love to sleep, you see, and I had pinned and mentally noted all the ways to remind our babies how to do it. Sleep was not going to be an issue for us.

Before reminding a baby how to sleep, I would have natural births. Of course. Any other way to have babies would be pumping them full of harmful CHEMICALS, and I would not be doing that to my babies. I will interject here and reassure all of you women who are mothers already and laughing at me that, no, none of this actually happened. Some of it, maybe, but most of it changed. So keep reading and don't be offended by my ridiculous parenting I did before I was ever pregnant.

I was an amazing mom before I had kids. My little Pinterest children ate all of their vegetables - which I painstakingly made into freaking works of art on their plates for each meal. They actually begged me for more broccoli and raw kale. My kids also wore the cutest clothes. I mean, every single piece was from a curated collection of modern designs. Not a cartoon character in sight.

I also had corresponding outfits for each of theirs. Which I effortlessly threw onto my bounced-back body and walked out the door. I buckled each kid into their HIGHEST POSSIBLE safety-rated car seat without a tear or cuss word from any of us. We went on outings about the town. Daily. Since I had learned to curl my hair and to do my makeup in between effortless and extended - but not creepily long - breastfeeding sessions, I looked like an actual model. We would go to the grocery store and each child could sit famously in the cart and clap for me as I added each item of produce into my cart. Passers-by would stop me and say, "Wow, your children are so beautiful and well behaved!" I would thank them and walk off in my heels. Then we would dash off to the next educational activity and we would all sing the ABCs on the way home for nap time. Yes, it was going to be awesome, and I knew exactly what I needed to know before any of it came to be.

Every so often people would ask us about babies; I didn't want to let on that I was counting down the minutes until Philip wanted to have them too. So I would act annoyed, but on the inside all I could hear was the ever-increasing ticking of my biological clock and the call of my uterus saying, "BABY! BABY! BABY!!!!" Regardless of whether or not he knew that's what I was doing, all of my probing and questioning - worked! And in the late summer of 2015, we began to have unprotected sex. I mean we pulled the goalie. I mean we started trying for a baby.

Chapter 4

GETTING PREGNANT

Patience has never been something I have been good at. It is still something I struggle with on a daily, nay, hourly basis in my adult life. When we started trying for a baby, I counted down the days and hours until I could finally take a pregnancy test. We had only been trying for one month, and I tried to tell myself it was going to be okay if it didn't happen this time. "Not everyone gets pregnant right away," I told myself. I finally felt like it was within the realm of reason to take a pregnancy test and bought as early of an early detection test as I could find. I tried to remain calm and positive, but of course I also thought, "If this is negative, I am going to be crushed." I went into my bathroom and peed on that sucker, full of anticipation. When I looked at the test TWO LINES appeared. Oh my gosh, the swirl of emotions that hit me. Bliss. Excitement. Fear. Panic. Holy crap, this baby is going to have to come out of me in some way or another.

Back when I was Pinteresting I had made mental notes of all the cute ways to tell your husband you are pregnant. There were a thousand different ways to do it, but in that moment when I saw the two blue lines, I could not hold it in anymore. Philip was in the backyard, and I ran outside and showed him the test. I showed him the test with tears welling in my eyes. "Babe! We are going to have a baby!" He was shocked but so excited. We hugged. We were both super excited, and I just remember walking around thinking, "There is a teeensy tiny little person in my belly! It worked, we made a person!"

I walked back inside and picked up the pregnancy test box and saw on the back of it that this particular test needed a + sign to be positive. I looked from the box to my test, from the box to my test and yeah...my two lines were actually one line short, and this test was in fact, negative. Whomp. Whomp.

That sounds maybe a bit callous, but I was actually really sad and I tried not to be devastated. It was early. There was still a chance, but I was pretty defeated. I might be slightly dramatic. A couple of days later I decided I just had to take another test. This time I read the instructions and knew what I was looking for. I peed on the stick and looked at the test. There wasn't a second pink line. But there also wasn't for sure NOT a line there. If you've ever taken a pregnancy test before, you know that when looking at a test your eyes tend to play tricks on you. I thought I saw a line; then in a different light, I didn't see a line.

I decided I needed a second opinion. I walked into the kitchen and showed Philip the test. Philip saw a line. He thought, "Ok cool; she is pregnant." I'm assuming. I don't know what he thought. But for me, well, I am a girl and I needed to know. Waiting for a missed period was not going to cut it. This was a lifelong dream here, friends. The next morning I ran into the bathroom to use the first urine of the day. Which apparently is like the golden ticket to finding out if you're pregnant or not. And this time I had bought a digital test. This was going to be a definitive test and I was not going to mess it up. I looked at the test and bolted into our bedroom.

I said, "THIS ONE IS POSITIVE!!! AND IT IS DIGITAL!!!"
Philip, who had been still sleeping, rolled over and said, "I knew it - my baby's having a baby!" So I was officially, officially pregnant.

The day after we found out, we went to a Detroit Tigers game and dinner with Philip's family. Philip and I were on cloud nine, but we did not want to tell anyone why. We kept looking at each other and smiling. Philip was sure to make sure I was always in the shade and had enough water. I think we slipped into this next stage of life pretty easily. It was smooth sailing, this pregnancy thing.

Being pregnant is actually one of my favorite things to be. Molly's pregnancy was relatively easy in the beginning, though it did have some challenges. I was nauseous, but I managed. At the time, I was working for a moving company - in the office - and the guys would come in at the end of the day and they would smell SO BAD. By no fault of their own, they were hard-working dudes. But the sweat and stale cigarette smoke made my pregnant stomach churn. That was one of the worst things about the first trimester: nausea. It hit me pretty quickly and lasted all day. The only things that really helped me feel better were Sprite and Pop Tarts. A very well-rounded nutritious snack. I was also beyond tired and would sometimes go to bed at 7:00. I tried to stay up later than that, but my eyes were just so heavy. On the weekend I would take a long, long nap. But that ain't a bad thing. This girl loves her some sleep. And Philip got to do things he normally wouldn't do while I was around, like watch a ton of sports and play PS4.

I had to keep this secret inside for what felt like years. But in actuality, it was only a few weeks. Maybe 6 weeks, I don't remember exactly. We had plans to go to my family's cottage for Labor Day weekend. Philip's family was coming and my family was coming. I remember it took for-ev-er for everyone to finally get there. We had bought two little bathing suits and I was somehow going to use that in the reveal. I also wanted to film it. But that was as much as I had planned. So when everyone was finally there, Philip and I went into the back of the house and strung the two bathing suits on a rope, I hit record on my phone and we just walked out into the living room where everyone was. In the moment it felt like 45 minutes until people noticed us. And then when they did see us, no one understood what was happening. My mom just said, "Ok, what's going on here??" and since she didn't immediately guess it right and I didn't really have a plan, I just stood there. Holding the string and my phone in my hand. SO AWKWARD. My heart was beating out of my chest and I had no idea what to do. Again, this felt like 20 years of standing there and staring. And FIN-A-LLY my sister Katie said, "Are you pregnant?" and I said, "YES!!!" And then everyone started crying and hugging us! Someone said, "How are you?" And I said, "Pretty nauseous." The video ends with a shot of my little nephew Tommy looking at my belly and his momma saying, "Your little cousin is in there." It is one of my favorite videos of all time. But it makes me sob every time I watch it.

Chapter 5

JOY AND SORROW

Let's fast forward again - I am trying to give you all the highlights of my motherhood journey. The highs and the lows, as you will see. But just the highlights. Y'all don't want my weekly fruit updates. And I don't want to go back and reread all of that stuff. Originally I was seeing a practice of hospital nurse-midwives. I was at my 18 or 20-week appointment; I can't remember which. But it was before I'd had any ultrasounds. You see, I wanted to keep my ultrasounds minimal so I wouldn't have a lot of false alarms or false diagnoses. Every week they used the doppler to find and check the baby's heartbeat, which is standard care. This particular day I happened to mention that I had already popped so much everyone thought I was having twins. The midwife then measured my fundal height and noticed I was measuring about 3-4 weeks ahead.

"Have you had an ultrasound yet?
"Nope, sure haven't."
"Ok... Has anyone ever picked up anything weird with the doppler before?"
"No. WHY?"

Saying something like this to me will always immediately cause 1,000 alarm bells to sound. Saying something like this to me whilst pregnant will immediately cause 6 trillion alarm bells to sound, and an overwhelming sense of panic started to creep into my heart.

"I think you might have twins. I can't tell for sure, but I think I was picking up two different heartbeats."

All I could picture were my two little chicken arms trying to carry two car seats, and I just about lost my mind. They didn't have an ultrasound machine or even a second doppler at their office. So another midwife came in and they tried to measure the heartbeats to see if what they were hearing was the same heartbeat or two different heartbeats; it could have been the cord, or they could have been picking up my heartbeat. The main midwife came in and told me I would be risking out of their practice if I had twins, but they could connect me with a great doctor that would allow me to try for a vaginal birth. The secretary got off the phone with the high-risk doctor and said the soonest they could fit me in was two weeks from then. TWO WEEKS. Yeah, that would be a solid no. Who could wait that long wondering if they were carrying two tiny people in their belly? We sure couldn't.

I called my sister-in-law and told her about it. I got so flustered that I got lost on my way back to work. If I could not do something as simple as driving to work, I was not going to be able to function for two weeks while waiting to find out - absolutely no way. I had to come up with a way to find out sooner. I called a local 3D ultrasound place to explain my situation. They are adamant on their website that they are for entertainment purposes only and do not diagnosis anything medical. Surely they would be able to diagnose twins though, right? I called and got their voicemail and left a pleading message. At work, I explained the situation to my boss and she just laughed and said, "You're so small, Mary." I know, and I am about to expand to the size of an elephant and then, potentially, push two watermelons out of a small opening.

Thankfully the ultrasound place called me back. They would be able to call it a "gender reveal" ultrasound, but their tech was fully trained and would be able to know if I was having one or two humans. Which, to be fair, I would hope whomever was operating their ultrasound machine for entertainment purposes or otherwise would be able to tell how many genitals they were looking for.

Phew.

I only had to wait a few hours before they could get me in and we would know. When 5 o'clock rolled around, Philip and I went to the ultrasound place and awaited our fate. To say we were on edge would be an absolute understatement. I laid down and lifted my shirt. They put the gel on my belly, which was actually warmed. I always saw on TV that they warn you it is going to be cold. Anyway, she started looking around and saw ONE BABY! I think we asked her a few times if she was absolutely sure. I had to make sure one wasn't just hiding behind the other one. Turns out there was just one.

She asked if we wanted to know the gender. We had briefly talked about waiting to find out at the birth. I think the relief of finding out there was only one let our guard down and we decided just to go for it. I asked if I could guess. I had no idea what I was looking at, so I took a stab in the dark and said, "Is it a boy?" "Nope, it's a girl!" The first thing out of my mouth was, "Oh no! I was terrible to my mother as a teenager!" and the second thing was, "That's Molly!" And then I started crying.

I had plans that night to see my mom, sister, and Philip's mom at a cooking party. When I got there, I gathered everyone around and told them it was a girl! It was one of the best parts of being pregnant. But soon after that, an event would happen that would change our lives forever. It was just the beginning of the hardest part of my pregnancy.

The very next day after finding out little Molly was brewing in my belly, we went to our last night of our birthing class. It was an hour or more long, and I didn't look at my phone the whole time. Once class was over, I looked at my phone and had a couple of missed calls from my mom and a text that said, "Call me please."

I instantly knew something was wrong. I called her and she told me my nephew, Tommy, had to get rushed to the ER. She didn't tell me a lot, but she said he was stable and they were going to run some tests in the morning. I remember being sick with fear and anxiety. So I just prayed and prayed and prayed and prayed.

For the rest of the evening, we tried to get ahold of everyone at the hospital. My mom assured me it would be okay and to just come in the morning to visit. I am not going to share every minute of that night with you. It is incredibly personal and incredibly hard for me to relive, and I just do not know if I can write it out and then edit it several times.

The short version of easily the worst night of my life is that Tommy passed away. He had Williams Syndrome and it affected his heart, as it does with all people with Williams Syndrome. And on that night, his heart just couldn't keep up anymore. He went to heaven to be with Jesus and his Grandpa Tom. Tommy forever changed me and everyone who ever met him. He emanated pure joy and brightened everyone's day. His favorite word was "hi," and he said it to EVERYONE he met. Tommy didn't know any strangers, just friends he hadn't met yet. I love that little boy; he made me an aunt, and he made me a better person. When we told our family we were pregnant, we got to go up north to our family cottage and spend an amazing weekend together. I will always cherish that weekend, not only because we told our family about our baby, but because I got SO many snuggles, 'hi's, hugs, laughs, and memories with Tommy.

This is an excerpt from a blog post I wrote at that time:
"As much as my heart aches and I can't imagine what my life could possibly look like from here on out - I am so grateful that our precious baby is on the way. Philip and I are so excited about the future, and we are just

honored and blown away that our baby has the same due date that Tommy had. And so, I will move on with this blog post as I move on each day, looking forward to the future but so glad for the memories."

The following days and weeks, months, years, and even up until today have been ebbs and flows of grief and holding onto his memory so tightly. It would have been his 5th birthday on April 12th, 2019, which is two days away from the time I am writing this. We are going to have a birthday party for him, and I am really glad we get to keep his memory alive and get to tell our kids about their cousin Tommy who lives in Heaven with their Grandpa Tom.

Chapter 6

PRENATAL CARE

In March of 2016, I came down with a stomach bug.

I was up all night running to the bathroom every few minutes. I'll spare you those details. I got dehydrated and I started having contractions. At the time I was roughly 30 weeks pregnant. Which is far too early to go into labor. I called the nurse hotline for my midwife practice, and they said to drink some water, take a shower, and if I had more than a couple contractions every 5 minutes then I needed to come in and make sure these were not progressing me into labor. To which I responded, "I've had two since I've been on the phone with you." So then I had to get up and go to the hospital.

I got to the hospital and went up to Labor & Delivery Triage. They hooked me up to all of the monitors and machines. Again, I was super dehydrated, so they had a hard time hooking up my IV; after several pokes, they finally got it in. One nurse (who actually plays a big role in this story, my birth story AND my second child's birth story - we love you Nurse Jenny) told me I would probably get some fluids and be on my way. Well, when I got hooked up to the monitors, my heart rate was through the roof - and so was Molly's. I also had a slight temperature. I tried explaining to them that I was pregnant, had a stomach bug, and was anxious because I was 30 weeks pregnant and in the hospital. But they figured something must be seriously wrong with me and decided they needed to run some tests.

I knew it was a stomach bug and not something else crazy, because just the weekend before, my sister had come over after my baby shower and spent the night at my house. In the middle of the night, she came upstairs and said, "I think I need to throw up," and then she did. A lot. And so on and so on. She has a condition called Hypoparathyroidism - yeah, say that 3 times fast - and if her calcium levels get too low she can go into seizures. I ended up calling my mom in the middle of the night because I did not know what to do. She answered on the first ring and drove almost an hour to my house, assessed the situation, and called an ambulance to come take her to the ER. She spent her birthday in the hospital with my sister because she is an incredible woman. So I told them, "I KNOW THIS IS THE FLU!" - but it was like flattening your towel on a windy day at the beach. Pointless and messy. And super annoying and gets sand in everyone's face.

I digress.

They thought maybe I had a blood clot which was causing the high heart rate. They asked if I had any calf pain recently. At the time I was eating like an actual garbage truck and was having charley horses left and right, so I decided to mention that. Well, the next thing I knew, Nurse Jenny was wheeling me down to get an ultrasound of my leg. No clot.

The mystery of why I had the fever was just baffling to them so I got admitted. I ended up staying in the hospital for 5 days and 1000 terrible nights' sleep. I had the worst heartburn ever, and I had to sleep basically sitting up. On the second or third night, I don't remember which, a nurse came in for rounds and lowered my bed all the way down and made me lay flat for an hour as lava crept into my throat whilst they monitored Molly. When she left, she hooked me back up to the heart rate and O2 finger monitors. This machine beeped all day and all night because I had a high heart rate. I asked her if she could turn the volume down and let me sleep, and she said "no" and turned and left. What a gem.

Prenatal Care

One morning the high-risk doctor came in with some residents to do rounds. One resident asked if I should get an amnio (a procedure in which they insert a large needle into your abdomen and puncture your womb to draw out amniotic fluid for testing, a procedure I am very much against and never dreamed of having) and the doctor scolded him and made him answer a bunch of questions about why that was a terrible idea. They decided to put me on a bunch of antibiotics to kill this "infection" and then meds around the clock to control my fever.

I went up and got a 30-week ultrasound the next day. I didn't really want one, but they made it seem like it was a good idea because of the high heart rate. Earlier in the pregnancy it was suspected that she had a heart condition, so we just decided to be safe and do it. I had the most lovely ultrasound tech and she talked us through everything. I get really chatty when I am nervous, but she was super pleasant and alleviated all of our fears. She said Molly looked great and we were good to go.

A couple of hours later the high-risk doctor and his students came in and said my fever was gone but my heart rate was still high so something had changed and I needed to have an amniocentesis. I did not want this to happen. Philip left the room to call my sister-in-law Laura and ask for her advice because she was well versed in this sort of thing. And also she's just really a great person to have around in a time of crisis. This is the very same sister-in-law who had lost her son a few months prior. She dropped everything and got in the car and came up to the hospital to advocate for me.

While Philip was on the phone with her, however, I was alone in the room, and a lot was going on. We had asked the doctors to give us some time to think about if we wanted to get this done. They thought that was absolute ludicrousy because my baby "might be in grave danger". So a nurse/resident guy came in and said he was going to draw my blood. I don't love getting my blood drawn, so I got nervous. As he stuck my vein and blood was starting to flow, his little doctor phone went off and he answered and said, "Uh huh. Ok. Yes. I will. Ok, sir," hung up and told the other nurse to get more vials for blood because they needed more labs. She ran out of the room to get more, as blood was somehow getting everywhere while he filled his vials. He said I needed to get an artery draw.

"A what??"
"So, instead of a vein, we need to stick the needle in deeper and draw directly from your artery. Everyone says it really hurts, but if you stay really still it won't be that bad."
"WHY?"
If you are a nurse. Or a doctor. Or a human being in the medical field I urge you never to say the following thing to a pregnant woman. Or a patient in general.

"Because he thinks you're really sick, honey."

And then I just lost it. I started sobbing and thinking something was wrong with me. He did the artery draw, and I stayed super still and it hurt, but it wasn't that bad; it was nothing like he described it was going to be. So that was done, but I was still flipping out. There were vials of blood everywhere, and he was not very accurate at containing the blood, and there was blood dripping everywhere; it was a whole scene. So then my precious and wonderful husband walks back in after being on the phone with Laura and sees blood and tubes and nurses and me sobbing and goes, "WHAT IS HAPPENING?!!"

I said, "They think I am really sick; I think I should get the amnio."

He obviously agreed because he had just walked into a war zone. You guys, looking back now, I feel like they played up that whole thing to get us to agree to the amnio. Maybe not, but it seemed like a whole hullabaloo to get us to do what they thought we needed.

So we get up to the ultrasound floor - the procedure is performed under ultrasound. Ya know, to make sure they don't stab your unborn child WITH A NEEDLE. But since this wasn't an actual emergency, and they knew it, I sat in the hallway for an hour waiting for my turn for an ultrasound to become available. While I was waiting, we saw the ultrasound tech who had done my scan that morning; when she saw me in the hallway, she came up and said, "What are you doing here??" We gave her a brief rundown of the events that had just happened. She seemed just completely shocked, because she had thoroughly looked over a perfectly healthy child but had to get back to work.

So when it was our turn for this "emergency" amnio, they started doing the procedure, and a resident was doing it, and he had to pull the needle out because Molly moved. At this point, the anxiety has started to really overcome me, and I have a minor fever from - let's say it together now - a stomach bug, so I got really hot, and the nurse got me a cold washcloth to lay on my head. The procedure happened relatively quickly, and it wasn't that painful. But when the doctor looked up, he saw the washcloth on my head and said, "What is wrong with you?"

Yeah, I just got a little nervous as you were putting a pointy object into my abdomen where my baby is. These people could write a book on how NOT to talk to patients.

They wheeled me back to my room and put me on constant fetal monitoring for four hours. They told me since there is probably something wrong, they are going to have to induce me and they will be moving me down to labor and delivery soon. Laura got there and stayed for several hours. She massaged me with oils, we talked, and she generally just took care of us. There was a shift change for nurses, and a new nurse came in and started taking my vitals. I asked her, "When am I going down to Labor & Delivery to be induced?" and she replied, "What? You're not getting induced!" So then she went on a mission to find out what was happening with me. She came back and told me so far everything from that morning was coming back normal, so they weren't going to need to induce me that day. This was at least 4 hours after the procedure, and nobody had bothered to come give me any of the positive or negative results. I was just hooked up to a monitor mentally preparing to have a baby that day.

At some point, my mom and her friend came up to the hospital to see me. Laura had gone home, and Philip wanted to go home to shower, get some clothes, and bring me some stuff back. As soon as he left, two nurses rushed into the room and told me to roll onto my side and started to turn on an oxygen machine. They told me the baby's heart rate had stopped and it wasn't coming back. I looked down at my stomach and said, "Well, the monitors have slipped off; could that be it?" "Oh, maybe." But just to be safe, they ordered an ultrasound at my bedside.

I also got several EKGs, labs, medicine, and they collected and tested my urine around the clock. It was a long 5 days, and finally they said if my fever stayed down on its own for 12 hours I could go home. I finally felt better - much like you do after you recover from a common illness - and took a shower and did my hair. I waddled out to the nurses' station and told them I wanted to go home, and if she didn't start the process I would just leave. She told me that if I did that, insurance wouldn't cover any of my bills. Friends, comrades, countrymen, THIS IS NOT TRUE. I don't know if she truly believed this or if she was just trying to get me to stay, but this is not fact. This actually comes up again years later, and I know for a fact it isn't true.

At some point, they thought I was good enough to go home and they went through the whole sign-out process with me. They gave me my discharge papers, and I was waiting for the wheelchair to come and escort me to our car. Then two lab techs came by the room and said:

48

Prenatal Care

"We're here for your lab work."

"Nope. I am going home; you must have the wrong person."

"Mary-Keith Piasecki? 9/22/88."

"Yes, that's me; it must be an old order."

"Nope, it was just put in."

"Yeah, no. I am not getting that."

Friends - you have a voice and a choice in your medical care - USE IT!

I have no idea why. Or how. Or what that was about, but it was thoroughly annoying. In my discharge paperwork somewhere deep down and hidden, they wrote that I was there for a STOMACH VIRUS. I cannot even. Or odd.

I got to go home and finally get some rest. After a few hours, I began to cry and told my husband, "I just can't stop worrying about Molly. What if I need more tests? What if she just isn't ok? They are making me doubt everything!"

I talked to my midwives at my next appointment. I told them how I didn't feel like anyone listened to me and I was bullied into a lot of things. I didn't think they knew what they were talking about. I didn't trust them, and I didn't want to go back to that hospital again.

So then we started looking for another provider. I was pretty late in the game and had no real leads on where to go or what to do. A friend of ours had a homebirth a few months before and had a great experience. So we started looking into that option. I interviewed a midwife at a birthing center and a homebirth midwife. Ultimately, we couldn't afford the birthing center, and they offered no additional medical equipment, so we decided to go with the homebirth midwife.

The rest of my pregnancy was pretty uneventful. I really enjoyed my prenatal appointments. My midwife was nice and we got along. She was pretty no-

nonsense. She had a lot of experience, and I felt like it was going to be great. One prenatal appointment I asked about pain. She basically told me that there were no pain management options at home. This was it.

Which, obviously, I understood that, but I just had never experienced labor before. So I was looking for some direction, guidance, reassurance, things of that nature. Of which there were none. I think she started to doubt that I was going to be able to do this.

Chapter 7

THE BIRTH OF MOLLY GRACE

Molly's due date was April 15th, and that day quickly came and went. Then I was a week late. Then I was 10 days late. All this time I had bouts of contractions that got closer but didn't grow in intensity. I thought I was going into labor FOR SURE for days. But they all died down. Then it was Tuesday, April 26th, 2016, 3:00 AM; I was awakened from my sleep with a strong contraction. They started coming 7-10 minutes apart, lasting 30-50 seconds for several hours. I woke Philip up and said, "These actually hurt - but I am not sure if this is it." He stayed home from work that day, and my contractions would pick up and then dwindle again. I couldn't sit down without a strong contraction radiating through my body. I tried to take it easy, in hopes labor soon would be here. Around 8 PM Laura, who was my doula for this birth, came over to take my mind off the disappointment of still being pregnant. She gave me a pedicure, rubbed my feet and hands with essential oils, and helped me relax. (Laura was incredible, by the way; this is not the last time you'll read about her selfless acts in this story.) By 11 PM my contractions were getting much stronger and I stopped being able to talk through them. I didn't want to say I was in labor, because I didn't want to say I was in labor when I really wasn't. Ya feel me? By 1 AM they were getting so painful that I decided this must be it. I was in full-blown labor. Or so I thought.

My photographer came a little after that and started snapping pictures. At this point, we still had Friends on in the background and I was listening to the dialogue and laughing to get me through the long contractions. I made everyone tell me stories to take my mind off the pain. Laura, Philip, and even my photographer pulled stories from every corner of their brains to help take my mind off contractions. My legs were getting tired from standing and swaying but every single time I sat down a fresh contraction would start.

Philip and Laura were constantly heating up rice packs and holding them on me to ease the pain in my back and my legs. Between each contraction, they held LaCroix and straw up to me so I would not get dehydrated.

My labor seemed to be progressing very quickly, and around 2:30 AM we called our midwife to come; I had stopped talking between contractions, and that was a sign that Molly was close to coming. I asked Philip to put some worship music on, praying that the power of the Holy Spirit would make the baby slip right out pain-free. (Spoiler alert: it didn't work.) I stood holding onto Philip to help get through contractions, I closed my eyes and prayed, I let the tears fall from my eyes. It was so peaceful; this is the birth I had imagined. This is how my baby was going to come into the world. This was my plan. This, however, was not Molly's plan.

I'd like to take a minute to do a shoutout to my husband here. Philip was amazing throughout this entire experience. I drew strength and courage from him, he quietly and confidently guided me through contractions.

After my midwife and her assistant got there, they started filling the birthing tub. I got into the tub for a while, and contractions just rocked my body. I started doing the labor moan they'd talked about in my birthing class. I thought, "This is it; my baby is going to come." I felt the need to push, and everyone was starting to get ready for her arrival. I started pushing, and nothing seemed to be happening. My midwife checked me and told me my body wasn't ready to push yet. This went on for what seemed like days. Contraction after contraction, feeling like I had to be making significant progress, and then being told that no progress had been made. At this point,

The Birth of Molly Grace

I was feeling pretty defeated.

Those contractions had hurt so bad, I was flopping around the tub like Shamu in a shallow pool. I asked my midwife why this was happening, and she tried to explain to me that I was scared and I needed to release into the process. From the couch, with her eyes closed, she would coach me and say, "You need to breathe down. Relax your face; you are scared." I didn't feel like she was in it with me. I didn't feel like she wanted this to happen for me. I knew Philip and Laura were all in and believed in me. But at that time what I needed was for her to tell me I could do it and that it would happen. I wanted some advice, some direction, an idea, perhaps, of what was going on. I had no idea what to do, and after around 3 hours in the birth tub, it was time to get out and try something different.

My contractions, unfortunately, were slowing down. After taking some time to rest during the lull in contractions, they finally started kicking in again consistently around 8 AM. At this point, I decided I was ready for the tub again, and I stripped down and got in. After laboring in there for another hour, I was checked for any progress; I was only at 6 cm. I labored and labored. She told me to give it another hour and then see what happened. She told me it was okay if I went to the hospital because some women just couldn't do it without pain meds. I didn't think I could do another hour; I didn't think I could do 5 more minutes. But the thought of getting dressed, driving in the car, getting checked into the hospital was horrifying. I was paralyzed with fear. I laid in the birthing tub and prayed out loud. Begging God to let me progress. And then, something clicked and I knew I needed to go to the hospital. I knew Molly wasn't in danger, but I just knew I had to go. My midwife was outside with her assistant moving back all of her appointments for the day. It was morning and they had been there all night without any real action.

After she came back inside, I told my midwife what I had decided, and she told me I needed to get up and get dressed by myself. I asked Laura if she would pack my bag while I got dressed; she said no. My midwife made moms in labor pack their own bags just to be sure that they were really serious about going to the hospital. I got myself out of the tub; someone handed me a towel, and I got to work.

I blindly grabbed sweatpants, shirts, underwear, socks, toiletries, baby clothes, anything that made sense to pack in between contractions. My birth team asked if I was sure, reminded me of what this entailed, but I was determined. Something (Someone) deep inside of me knew I needed to do this.

I yelled at my poor husband; he tried to tell me I could do it. He tried to get me to stay, but I yelled at him that I was not going to. Laura told me I couldn't talk to her that way, but also told me to stick it out. At that point I was in so much pain, and it didn't seem like it was ever going to end, so I told her I was done. I learned later that my midwife had told her that I should go to the hospital because I had given up. So they let me go.

We got in the car, and contractions got stronger and closer together. I tried desperately to get ahold of the hospital midwives, my previous care providers, but to no avail. We pulled up to the ER entrance as another contraction hit, and I birth-warrior-roared my way into the security line. The security guard told me to go past the line and got me a wheelchair. Someone else asked me stupid questions like, "How far apart are your contractions?" "How many weeks are you?"
"I HAVE BEEN IN LABOR FOR 30 HOURS, I AM 6 CM DILATED, AND MY DUE DATE WAS 12 DAYS AGO!" and off we went to triage.

They rolled me into triage and Lyric the triage nurse-midwife said, "Mary-Keith?"
"I HAVE BEEN IN LABOR FOR 30 HOURS, I AM 6 CM DILATED, AND I NEED SOME FREAKIN PAIN MEDS!" I politely responded. She got me past triage and into a room without getting hooked to a monitor.

The next few minutes is honestly a fog. During one particular contraction, I stood up out of my wheelchair in such a fashion that Philip said it looked like a scene from The Ring. He thought I would have given myself a C-section if a scalpel was nearby. I insisted on walking to my room on my own, screaming about wanting pain meds. I was the picture of grace and poise.

In my labor room, they told me I needed to strip down and get into a robe in order to get an IV. Within 10 seconds I was stark nude with both arms held straight out - waiting for them to pick any vein they needed. Then I had to sign paperwork - I am pretty sure I signed the rights to my second born and the deed to my house over. Didn't matter - this meant relief was coming. They got my fingerprints in record time. Literally, they told me no one had ever done their fingerprints faster.

It was at that moment I remembered that I had thrown away my physical birth plan in an act of defiance because I was having a home birth, suckas! But when I needed it, I didn't have it.
So I started yelling out things I remembered from my birth plan: "I want skin to skin when she's born!" "No Pitocin!" "No Hep B!"

They checked me and I had progressed to an 8. Finally, progress. Must it have been in the car and while stomping around a hospital? Apparently. Then I finally got the pain meds. Glory be. After 10-15 minutes the drugs began to set in, and I was able to get some relief. I started to relax a bit, and I started to progress. I labored for a few hours and got to a 9. After I got to a 9, I started to stall again. I was in so much pain, and I was so incredibly tired. But I had to keep going; this baby had to come out.

Eventually, I felt like I needed to push again, but I wasn't ready. I'd had enough; I wanted the epidural. Everyone thought I could keep going, that Molly was almost in my arms, but I knew in my head I could not do this without a break. So I asked for the epidural. An epidural was something I said I never ever wanted. I am afraid of needles, I am weirded out by my spine being touched - so the combination of the two was just something I could never do. But that little voice inside of me told it was time for a break.

Philip encouraged me that it was okay, I needed this, I had put in the time, and it was not giving up. Getting the epidural was hard. I was still having contractions, and I felt like I was weak for getting it. I wept as they had me hunch over a pillow and the doctor performed the procedure. They laid me on my back and let the medicine do its magic.

I want to take a quick pause here and talk about how amazing my nurse was. Remember Nurse Jenny from the original hospital stay? While I was getting hooked up to IVs, none other than Nurse Jenny walked in. I think she was glowing like an angel. She was definitely a sight for sore eyes. She had my back when I was in the hospital the first time, and it was like a sigh of relief seeing her smiling face walk into my room. Ya know, honestly, I might have verbally sighed when I saw her. Or something classy and low-key. But that is not true. I sat up and pointed at her and said, "I KNOW YOU!" Thankfully she said she remembered me too and was excited she got to be at my birth. It felt like a celebrity was in the room with me. I had an amazing team of supporters at the hospital with me, but Nurse Jenny was different because this was her turf and she was on my team. So in the "land of the unknown," I had at least one player on my team. The midwife on call that day was named Nicole. I had actually never met her, but when she walked in and started talking to me, I liked her right away. She is a natural midwife, as in the profession of midwifery comes naturally to her I believe. She cares about her patients and knows her stuff. I learned all of this in the 10 hours I was with her that day. And in the years following I consider her a friend. I actually felt like she heard me, and she TOLD ME she wanted me to have this baby the way I wanted and she would help me get there. Both of these women stayed with me the whole time I labored because they are champs.

About 10 minutes after getting the epidural, I started feeling really loopy and relaxed. I had the break that I had been begging God for. I got to eat some popsicles; I cracked jokes, laughed, texted a few people to update them, and built up my confidence. An hour later I was finally fully dilated and got the okay to push! I pushed and I pushed; I barely felt a thing. This was glorious. Drug-Free is NOT the way to be. After about 1.5 hours I started to feel pain and pressure in my back and bum. They checked and did not think she was in an optimal position. I got on my hands and knees, I squatted, I laid on my back, I did everything I could think of to turn her.

I want to pause here and talk again about Laura. She held my legs, rubbed my back, held me up while I squatted with everything in me. She showed me a selfless love I had never experienced before. She poured herself out for me hour after hour; I would not have been able to get through if it weren't for her.

Okay, back to the story... Here I am like Salt N Pepa, Pushin' Real Good. Times are a blur but over the course of about 2 hours, they checked me a few times and she went from +3 to +1 (which is moving backward). I would start to feel the intense back pain, and then it would be relieved.

The doctor came in to give her opinion: Molly had plenty of room to get out, but she was wiggling backward and turning herself sunny side up. It seemed to me someone should have realized she was sunny side up long before this. No one had, and so I was in the 300th hour of labor and was super hungry, really tired and just not ready to continue the battle.

I was so defeated again. I felt like I was running a race in sinking sand and losing. Nicole told me to let the doctor try to manually turn her, that if this one thing could've worked and I didn't try, I would regret it. So I agreed. During the next contraction, they told me to "get mean" and push with all I had. So as a contraction rocked through my back and my butt, I pictured every nay-sayer I had encountered about my home birth. They would not be right. I was big enough, tough enough, I could do this, I WOULD do this. With 8 fingers (that's a full hand and some change) the doctor turned Molly to the correct position. I screamed a scream that would scare small children and grown men alike. Philip thought his brain was going to melt.

After it was over they checked me a few minutes later. She had already begun to turn herself. I. Was. Done.

I told them I wanted a C-section. I would not be able to do this. I was so tired, everything hurt so bad, and I just wanted my baby. They said she had room, I could keep going, I could do it, her heart rate never faltered, her stats were good, but she might just keep turning herself. They offered other ways to help get her out. That was met with a quick "NO!" and a finger wag.

So a C-Section it was. They said it typically takes 30 minutes from when they order the C-Section to when we're in the OR. Those 30 minutes felt like 3 hours. I cried, I felt like a failure, I didn't want my birth team to be mad at me. I thought they would think they wasted all their time with me. We had come this far just for me to give up. Laura looked at me with tears in her eyes and told me I had earned this, I had done more than enough, and it was okay.

Eventually, I think because of my swearing, threats, and attempted bribes, the anesthesia team came in. She asked on a scale of 1-10 what my pain was. "50!" She then bent the rules and started the drugs just a little before we got to the OR. Praise the Lord for that woman.
The pain meds were flowing, I was feeling better; soon after, they fully numbed me, and Philip got to come in.

The sensations one feels during a C-section can't be fully described. It's just weird. They pulled me open, pulled out my insides, rearranged them, and put them back in. The first thing the doctors saw when they cut open my womb was Molly's eyes staring straight up at them. In just over half an hour, she had managed to flip over yet again. Then the doctor said, "Is Dad in here?" "I'm here." "Stand up, Dad." And boom, she was out. They walked around the corner with her in their arms, and I saw my little baby for 1 second. Then they left to check her vitals. They started putting me back together, and I started to cry. They asked if I needed more meds, and I said, "I'm not crying because it hurts, I am crying because I'm a mom now."

While they were examining Molly, they noticed her breathing sounded off, so they pulled Philip aside and had him look at her and told him they needed to take her upstairs. They asked for his consent to give her formula. This was not something we ever even thought about for one second, so he said yes. And off she went to the NICU.

I was extremely groggy and out of it, and I asked Philip many times, "Where is she? Is she ok??" Philip always told me yes even though I would find out later he didn't know if she was okay and was really worried about her. I got wheeled into recovery and was still out of it. Nurses were in and out, and I don't remember much of what happened. I know at one time I sent Philip to go check on Molly who was in the NICU. While he was gone alarms went off, and somewhere in the hospital there was a code. I flipped out and thought it was Molly. Philip got up to her, and they showed him his daughter. She had oxygen on and a tube down her nose. They were pumping fluid out of her. Other than that, she seemed totally fine. The nurse who was taking care of Molly said the way they described her, she thought a really sick baby was coming up, but Molly was perfectly healthy. Hospital policy is to keep babies that come to the NICU in the NICU for at least 24 hours.

Back down in recovery, nurses were telling me that Molly had something called Tracheomalacia and she would likely need reconstructive surgery because her trachea hadn't fully formed. So when Philip arrived back down with a picture of Molly and telling me she was totally fine - I can't even begin to tell you the relief that washed over me. And then annoyance, because yet again people were telling me the worst-case scenario without fully knowing the facts. After I had been in recovery for several hours, they told me I could go up and meet my daughter. I had been under heated blankets since after surgery, so I was really hot and they thought I was running a fever. Nurse Jenny had gone home and my new nurse told me it wasn't likely that I would be able to hold my daughter because of "how sick she was." In cases like mine, babies never get held the same day they are born.

I just want to cut in here again and say - IF YOU ARE A NURSE: Please get your facts straight before you talk to a patient. You can 100% make or break the experience of your patients. I understand that there is a lot about nursing that I do not understand. There are a lot of cooks in the kitchen, but it seems to me that before you make such a declarative statement you need to be sure that what you are talking about is a fact not a "maybe."

When I got wheeled into the NICU and I saw Molly swaddled up and laying in the crib, from the way she was kicking her legs, I knew she was mine! I said, "That's her! That is what the kicks felt like from the inside!" Then they just plopped a baby in my arms. It was surreal. She was so tiny and, like, mine. She had oxygen on, but she looked like a little cherub baby. She was our baby. I loved her so much. I kissed her little head, but it had a hat on it. So I kissed her little face.

And my nurse said, "Don't kiss her; you have a fever, and we don't know why." So I ignored her and kissed my baby anyway.

So, nothing can prepare you to be a new mom. I didn't know what to do with her quite yet. She had already been fed formula, so she didn't need to eat. And there was a group of nurses staring at us. So when they told me I had to leave, I was like, "Ok, sounds good." I didn't feel this instant bond to her. I didn't think I couldn't be away from her, because I didn't even know how to be with her. Laura offered to sit in the nursery with her all night so she wouldn't be alone. She said she wouldn't hold her, she would just be there so she had someone. Which in hindsight, I would absolutely accept if it were to happen again. But again, I had no idea what to do with her or how to feel. So I told her the nurses would be fine and she could go home.

The next morning, after an excruciatingly painful trip to the bathroom, I asked if I could go see Molly again. And they were like, "Yeah, she's your baby!" Oh yeah...like, I am her mom and I get to decide these things. Crazy.

I'll speed things along here a bit. Our families came up and met her and held her. I got to try and nurse her for the first time. Which was really, really hard. I had no idea what I was doing. The NICU nurses kept giving her formula, so maybe she wasn't that hungry. And breastfeeding is just really hard, and it takes time and effort for both you and the baby to figure it out. Eventually, I got moved to a different room, and Molly was released from the NICU and got to stay with us.

I remember this conversation with a resident who came in and did rounds.

"So, you tried to have a home birth?"
"I did. But after she wasn't coming, I decided to come in."
"You know you can NEVER have another home birth again now. After you've had a C-section, you will die if you try again."
"I just had a baby one day ago. I am not even sure if I want more kids."
"Just know that home birth is not an option for you."

This delightful resident actually comes back into my life later on. She is another gem. *Sarcastic Smile*

We got released from the hospital, and they just gave us this baby and were like, "This is yours; good luck!"

Chapter 8

BABY MOLLY

You guys. Having a newborn is hard. I am going to insert a blog post I wrote at this time. It pretty much sums up my feelings about the newborn phase.

"Molly is 1 month old! I'd like to sit here and say, "It went by so fast!" But it didn't. It feels like months, not just one. Philip and I agree - it feels like I was in labor last year. We're both exhausted. We knew it was going to be hard; we knew we would be up at all hours of the night. But no one can prepare you for it. You can't be prepared.

"Parenthood is hard. These 4 weeks have been long and tiring. We have given and given to this tiny little human and she has sucked (literally) everything out of us. I have come to the end of myself many, many times. I have cried in the middle of the night because I have been so tired. I have cried in the middle of the night because my nipples were raw and she was hungry. I have cried in the middle of the day because she's crying and spitting up and I can't get a good burp out of her. I have cried because I dread going to bed every night because nights are long. I have felt guilty because I am not enjoying this. I have felt guilty because I have missed my old life. I have felt guilty because I do not want to feed her again. I have been mad because she spit up on me, again. I have been annoyed that I have to change her, again. I have felt guilty that I just want her to be able to hold her head up, or smile, or say DaDa!

"But then - I have cried because I have an overwhelming and crippling love for this teensy tiny human. I have stared at her face and begged God not to let her grow up. I have kissed her tiiiny little cheeks over and over because I just love her so much I could eat her up. I have kissed her head and inhaled that baby smell in the middle of the night and it makes my heart swell.

"So I'll be honest - this newborn phase is hard. It is not enjoyable; she gives almost nothing back. But there is something so special and cool about knowing that I can give her comfort that no one else can. Philip and I are keeping her alive; we are being parents. It is awesome.

So, Molly, if you ever read this, know that we love you more than we ever thought possible. Know that the first month of your life felt like years, but I am sure we will look back and think it flew by. Know that you made us parents and we will always be grateful for that. You have stretched us in ways that we never thought possible. You have already increased our dependence on the Lord an exponential amount. We are stronger as a couple because of you; we are better people because of you."

After a while the newborn phase ended. Everyday got a little bit easier. This is not to say that having kids is easy. Every stage has ups and downs. But it is incredible what you can do when you are sleeping a bit more.

Philip and I fumbled our way through early parenthood. We learned a lot - one thing we learned is that you will talk, think, and worry about poop more than you ever did in your entire cumulative years before kids. This happened to both Philip and me on separate occasions. We would change Molly's diaper, and since she is a girl, we didn't think much about quickly getting another diaper on her. Then she decided this was a great time to poop. And she would fire off so hard that it hit the opposite wall in the nursery. You guys that is poop. Liquid poop. It sprayed out of her and HIT. A. WALL. It hit the changing table and the clean clothes and clean diapers. Nothing was spared from the wrath of her bowel movement. What do you do in that situation? You scream. You look around and realize you are the parent in that situation and you wildly try to clean it up.

When Molly was about 5 months old she started pooping once a week. She was 100% breastfed and it was on the scale of normal - I learned from the Googles. But every time she pooped it was like a whole event. We knew it was coming; it was usually a Saturday, and she would be sort of fussy and super gassy all day. Then her little face would get red and a concerned look would come over her, and she would just let it all out. It would go from her head to her knees, and then we would clean her up and wait for the next one the next week.

One time I was recording myself singing and dancing while she sat in the bumbo seat. Mind you, I cannot sing, nor can I dance very well, but I was cracking her up and I wanted to capture those giggles. A few seconds into the video, her face got red and she filled up her diaper. Since she was in a seat, it sounded like a rocket was taking off.

When Molly was 6 months old we went to Florida for vacation. I won't lie; I don't like traveling with babies. I don't love flying to begin with, and the stress of getting through the airport and on the plane and worrying if she is sleeping enough or eating enough is a lot. Then there's the whole thing of getting them to sleep in different places. Remember how I was this Expert Pinterest Mom? Well, I had read all of these tips and tricks on how to travel with babies. But when push came to shove, I couldn't get her to nap or sleep in the same room as us. I did my best to make the most of it. I also had postpartum anxiety and I hated leaving her with anyone other than my husband. I trusted people, but Anxiety told me it wasn't going to be okay. So this trip was fun, but I had a lot of emotional hurdles to jump over, and I have a hard time looking back at that trip and looking at the good parts of it. So back to poop.

The day we were leaving on our way back home, we realized she hadn't pooped yet. Our fear was that she would decide to poop on the airplane and then we would have to clean her in an airplane bathroom. I did all the Googling I could do to find things to encourage her to poop. Massaging her tummy, kicking her legs, you name it. One site I read said it would help get her going if you stimulated her bum hole. I consulted with every Facebook mom group, and many moms said they had done the same thing. So we laid her down on the bed. Prepared the area for the poo-splosion that was about to happen. Got a Q-tip, dipped it in coconut oil, and uhhhh, put it in her bum. And I mean, it did not even go in one centimeter. And not even for one second. And then we waited. Nothing happened.

So we did it again. And nothing.

We had no choice but to go to the airport, and we hoped that she would just wait until we got home. But she didn't. We were going down the road, and her face got red. Philip and I looked at each other knowing what was happening. After she finished pooping she started crying. Poor girl. We pulled over at a gas station to assess the damage. And it was vast. My mother-in-law took her clothes inside and tried to clean them in the sink. We held Molly up naked like a certain Disney lion cub and gave her our best bath with baby wipes. The whole time we just kept laughing. This is stuff no one tells you about. This is the stuff that you just figure out as you go.

Chapter 9

HAVING ANOTHER BABY?

Philip and I never wanted to have 2 kids under 2. For whatever reason, that just seemed completely not doable. Too hard, too much work. Not going to happen. I doubted many times if I ever wanted to have another one. But as soon as I put Molly's 12-month clothes away in storage, baby fever hit me. Molly was old enough that the threat of having two under two was over, so we decided to start trying. Now if you remember, Molly happened one month after we had started trying. I knew that this might not happen again the second time. But I really thought and hoped that it would. After the first month, I didn't get pregnant. Or the second. Or third. I immediately gave up hope. I started thinking it was never going to happen. Much like when I was waiting forever for Philip to propose (read: 8 months), I just have no patience when there is something in front of me that I want. I know that many people wait years and years to get pregnant. I tried to keep it in perspective, but sometimes I am the worst.

During those four months, I easily spent $100 or more on pregnancy tests. I would try and wait until I missed my period. I really would. But each time there was a chance the test would be positive, I would go out and buy an early detection test. And those are not cheap. When those tests would come back negative, I would wait a few more days and then test again. Each time, I would be devastated and somewhat hopeful that the next test would be the one to tell me the good news. Until my period came, and then I would cry a few tears. One time, I even got my phone out and started recording because I just knew this was going to be the positive test. The camera focuses on the test that reads "NO," I laugh, and shut off the camera.

This went on for three months. And each month, I would cry and tell Philip that I was just sure it wasn't going to happen. Then I would remind myself that I was blessed to have one child and it was going to be okay no matter what happened. I really did, but I was still a basketcase every month. At the time, I was still nursing Molly. Molly never took a bottle and primarily nursed until she was a year old. Then she slowly began having solid food. She was a comfort nurser, and whenever she got a bump, was scared, or got tired she would want to nurse. It was also her way of falling asleep at night. You read that correctly; I nursed her to sleep. And she slept 12 hours. So let's all just calm down.

So I was still nursing my 17-month-old, and I was training for a CrossFit competition, so I was doing a hard workout five days a week. I think my body was like, "Yeah, no. We are not taking on another human right now." A couple of weeks later, I was ready to be done nursing Molly because she was starting to want to nurse because she was bored and I couldn't handle it anymore. I also pulled a muscle in my neck and had to back off training. The very next month, I got pregnant. I was taking test after test. I was posting in my favorite mommy Facebook group (Shout out to all my girls in HA Alumni Moms!), and they were being super encouraging to me. I posted a picture of my pregnancy test, and a few of them said it was positive. I still had my doubts. I really needed to be sure, because I did not want to be crushed again. I went to my family's Thanksgiving, and the whole time I kept thinking, "Am I pregnant? IS THIS HAPPENING?" The next day I did another test, and this one was clear-as-day positive. And that was it. I was pregnant again.

Chapter 10

HAVING ANOTHER BABY

We really wanted to wait to tell our families. I knew once I told my mom I was pregnant, all of her friends and my aunt would know. Despite her "Who am I going to tell? I have no one to tell" story that she tells every.single. time I try to tell her a secret, somehow soon thereafter I get, "Well, I only told so and so..." So knowing that when we told her, it would no longer be a secret, we waited. A little while.

Just a few weeks after I had Molly, I began my research into having a Vaginal Birth After Cesarean (VBAC). I had been researching for well over a year and knew beyond a shadow of a doubt that I wanted to have one. [I won't get into it here because you probably are not here to read about statistics and the history of VBAC - though let me tell you, it is fascinating. Basically after reading books, studies, forums, and personal testimonies, then finding Dr. Stuart Fishbein's podcast, I just knew I wanted a VBAC and felt it was a safe option for me.] Listen; long story short, our bodies were made to have babies, and if you have a provider who knows what to look for and won't push the limits, then VBAC is totally possible. Ok, now I am done, really.

Within my research for VBAC, I started studying to become a birth doula. I had received such amazing care and support during Molly's labor - from my sister, my husband, nurses, and nurse-midwives - that I just wanted to be that person for other mommas who didn't have those options. The slogan for my doula business is "you needn't walk alone." This is just such a strong theme in my life; it breaks my heart to think about anyone going through pregnancy, labor, birth, the newborn phase, or any phase in motherhood - or really even just being a woman - without someone walking by her side.

Once I got the positive test, I knew my plan of action. I was going to interview Jill to be my montrice. Who is Jill? What is a montrice? Great questions. Jill is a midwife who also works as a montrice and a doula. I had interviewed her during my first pregnancy. She worked at the birth center that I could not afford, but I had met her previously and really liked her. She also caught a few of my friends' babies and came very highly recommended to me in the birthing world. A montrice is basically between a doula and a midwife. In fact, they're actually recommended for VBACs. Doulas do not do anything medical at all. They're there for moral, emotional, and physical support. They advocate for you and your birth plan, but they do not make any choices for you. Midwives are there for medical support, and if they're amazing, they're there for the emotional side too. A montrice will provide some medical services, such as cervical checks and checking on the baby's heart rate, before you go to the hospital, then switch gears and solely be your doula at the hospital. I knew I wanted a hospital birth, but I wanted to labor as long as I could at home, so a montrice was the way to go.

I met with Jill at her office, and I brought Molly with me. Jill got her some toys to play with, and Molly felt at ease with her right away. She did not cling to me like she normally did and played quietly on the floor while Jill and I chatted. She was and is the sweetest and most comforting woman I have ever met. She slowly rocked in her rocking chair, and I told her my fears about having a homebirth and asked her if she would be my montrice. She wanted to know about my home birth and listened while I explained my story in great detail. She nodded or shook her head at all of the right places. She asked me if I would consider a homebirth again. I thought maybe she had not heard me right. I said no way, that I was not going to have this baby at home. I had been down that road and failed, and some women just can't get through labor without pain meds. I am one of those women, so I don't want to try.

She compassionately went on to explain that I didn't fail at my first birth; I was failed by someone. I was not supported, and my midwife probably should have known Molly was ill-positioned weeks ahead of time. She thought I had it in me to do it at home. "But what about uterine rupture?" I asked, even though I knew from my research that uterine rupture was super rare. "I know the signs of rupture, I know what to look for; I would know well ahead of time if there was a problem." "Ok, sure, sure. But is this safe?" "You know I wouldn't put you in a dangerous situation for fun. If you got hurt or the baby got hurt, that would affect me negatively in many ways." She met each fear with facts and experience. Talking to Jill is remarkable; she is the smartest and sweetest woman. But she isn't in your face about her knowledge; she only shows her cards when you ask her a question. And the confidence but complete and total care in her voice when she talks to you, it's like talking to your mom or best friend. She just sees into your soul and gets you.

At this point in the meeting, Molly started pooping. I say this because Molly was weird about her poop at this stage and usually waited until she was in the comfort of her own home to relieve herself. She looked at me with a red face and mouthed, "I'm poopin'," and you guys, I took that as a sign. A sign that if Molly was comfortable enough with Jill to poop around her, then I should be too. I mean have a baby around her, not poop around her. But - spoiler - both of those things happened.

I left that meeting reconsidering and actually sorta wanting to have a home birth. Now I needed to get Philip onboard. My husband is amazing; I'll say again and again that he trusts me and he said if it was safe and what I wanted to do, then he would do it. So we met with Jill again. And I think I asked her the same questions, and Molly pooped AGAIN. She was doing her best to be like, "MISS JILL IS THE BEST!" We walked out of that meeting deciding to have a homebirth. Jill not only has the confidence, skill, knowledge, and experience to back up her claims, she is really, really kind and compassionate and just lovely to be around.

We were so excited about our choice to have a home birth, that we decided we were going to tell our families that very night (about the baby, NOT the home birth). From Jill's office, we drove down to the mall to meet Philip's family for dinner. We had even less of a plan than we did when telling them about Molly. We just knew when there was an opportunity to bring it up, we would just tell them. So in the middle of dinner, I asked them, "Do you guys have any plans in July?" They sort of laughed and said they weren't really sure, and we said, "Well, we are going to be having a baby." Not super elaborate, but it worked. They were so surprised and excited for us! I loved watching everyone's faces as the realization washed over them! After we hung out with them for a bit, we called my mom and stopped in at her house. She didn't think anything of it, since we were in the area. We chatted for what felt like hours, and then I asked her what she was doing in July. She said, "Well, I usually get about a week off..." And continued on and on about her summer plans. Which I had just asked her about, but was not expecting a full rundown. I could not take the anticipation anymore and just blurted out, "We are going to be having a baby in July!" Her mouth dropped open in total shock. It was super sweet. I thought we had been painfully obvious with our sudden stop in, but thankfully we hadn't! We didn't ruin the surprise at all!

I loved telling our families when we were going to have babies. Actually, telling people about being pregnant is one of my favorite parts about being pregnant. Our first social media baby announcement featured our dog and the game Settlers of Catan. Our second baby's post was a Boomerang of us throwing confetti and the caption said, "Happy New Baby" as an ode to Gilmore Girls. If you know, you know. Even with all the excitement, there is always a twinge of sadness. Sadness that my dad isn't there to celebrate with us. I wish my dad was here and could meet his grandbabies. I wish I could see them interact with their Grandpa Tom. I think of my dad holding my younger cousins when they were babies, and I get a lump in my throat thinking about all the baby snuggles he never got to have. I also think about Tommy and how I wish wish wish with all my heart he was here to meet his cousins. I wish my kids got to know him and love him. I now have to try and explain to Molly where Grandpa Tom and Tommy are and why they can't come to her house. She knows they are in Heaven; she knows to get there you have to be dead, but she has no concept of what that truly means. That they won't be better when she is 4. Or maybe they can be there for the 4th of July, for some reason that is the date she has picked out in her head as when they will be "better." It's hard to have those conversations with her over and over. But I also love that she knows who they are and that she can pick out their pictures and say confidently who they are. There is joy mixed with deep grief in each big moment in my life. I think there always will be.

We were aware that after my family found out, a lot of other people were going to know. The thing that we decided to try keeping under wraps as long as we could from everyone, even our families, was that we were going to have a home birth. First of all, people think home birth is crazy enough as it is. Second, having a VBAC at home is like telling people you think aliens are going to deliver your baby. And thirdly, I had already tried this and failed, so if I wasn't able to do it for the second time, I would be super embarrassed. So we did our best to keep it to ourselves.

Part of why we love Jill was that she did not accept us as a client just for our money. She actually believed I could do it, she wanted me to do it, and she made sure we were going to be a good match before she took me on. After I told her my first birth story and how crazy and not peaceful it was, she gave me two requirements to be her client. I had to take a hypnobirthing class, and I had to hire the doula she suggested. My first birth wasn't very peaceful but she believed that my next one could be, nay, that it would be as long as she could help it.

Having Another Baby

Each of my prenatal appointments was like a mini-vacation or trip to the spa. I loved hearing the baby's heartbeat, and Jill always answered any questions I had. She would reassure me about any fears I had that particular day, because there was always something I was worried about. I had absolutely no appetite throughout my first trimester. I tried to make myself eat protein and good fat-filled foods, but I just never wanted to eat. I was not really gaining much weight and was nauseous all day and all night. I never threw up though; I just felt like I was on the verge of it all the time. I told Philip I could never do this again, it was too much. Jill was concerned with my lack of weight gain because I just wasn't gaining anything. But Baby continued to grow, and I continued to try to eat. The only relief I had was working out. I had already been doing CrossFit, and I got the approval to keep going so long as I listened to my body. The endorphin rush at the end of the workout was enough to keep my nausea at bay for a couple of hours. I ended up doing CrossFit throughout my whole pregnancy except for the final couple of weeks.

Toward the beginning of my pregnancy, I found out that none other than Joanna Gaines was pregnant too. If you know me at all, you know I love me some JoJo. This really was just the icing on the cake of pregnancy.

Chapter 11

THE UNKNOWN

My brother-in-law lives in the Middle East. It is quite the commute when he comes home to see us, and we miss him a lot while he is gone. But he loves it there and wants to stay there, so we have accepted it. When I was pregnant with my second baby, he got engaged. They decided to get married where they live because they love it there so much. I had gone back and forth about whether or not I was going to go to the wedding, but ultimately decided not to. It was going to be a quick trip, just one week. And about 40 hours of traveling. I was pregnant and did not want to travel that far for that short of time if I wasn't going to get any rest. Once they got to their destination, they hit the ground running in full wedding prep. We didn't want to leave Molly and go that far away either. We hadn't yet left her for more than one night at a time. And even then, she was only 25 minutes away from us. The thought of her being oceans away was too much. And bringing her with us sounded like pure torture. For everyone involved. So we made the choice for Molly and me to stay back. Even though Philip was going to the safe part of the Middle East, that's like telling someone you're going to the safe part of Detroit. It's still the Middle East, and it is still scary and unknown. I just imagined his plane crashing into the sea. Or while he was there for the wedding, getting bit by a camel then getting some crazy sickness and then he would have to stay there - thousands of miles away - for an unknown amount of time. There were just going to be so SO many miles between us, and that just left a lot of room for error.

The day before Philip boarded the plane for the wedding, we had our anatomy ultrasound at 18.5 weeks. Ultrasounds actually make me really nervous because they have the potential to find something wrong. Even though it is better to know if something is wrong, I still got nervous that they would find something. When I was pregnant with Molly, they thought they found a very serious heart condition, and after several stressful appointments and extra ultrasounds, it turned out to be absolutely nothing. But at this appointment, we were also going to find out the gender of the baby. I'll be honest; I really, really wanted a boy. I was preparing to have a girl, because I wanted a boy so badly. Molly is great, but I wanted Philip to get his mini-me... and I wanted to not have to raise another girl. During the ultrasound, we mentioned a few times that we wanted a boy. The ultrasound tech couldn't get a good view, which worried me. If she couldn't see anything, maybe that meant there was nothing to see. She said she had a guess, but wouldn't tell me until she was sure. As she looked around, she told us the baby was super healthy and everything was great on the ultrasound. It was time to try to look at the gender again.

"Oh, man. I think I know what it is..." I said, with clear disappointment in my voice.
"I know what you're thinking, but you're wrong... there is the penis."

Silence.

"..What!?! It's a boy!?!?"
Philip and I just sat in stunned silence. Jill had enough of that and joyfully chimed in, "Well, if you aren't going to hug her I am!!"

We were both just so shocked. We came in hoping for a boy but prepared for a girl! We were sooo excited! But the second she told us it was a boy, all the names we had picked for a boy sounded terrible and we had no idea what to name him.

Once we found out he was a boy, we got to tell everyone our little secret again. It was so fun, and people's reactions are always so different. We told our families that day via some simple phone calls, and I believe I just texted my friends, "WEINER!" Because I am a classy lady.

When Philip got in the car to go to the airport the next day, I couldn't keep the tears from falling. I miss him so much when he is away, and he was going to be farther away from me than we had ever been in our lives, including even the time before we knew each other, and my pregnant emotions could not handle that thought. To keep our minds off the fact that Daddy was so far away, my in-laws bought Molly and me tickets to go to Florida for the week. We were going to stay with Philip's aunt who lives along the Intracoastal Waterway in Florida. We found a direct flight from our little local airport to the little local airport in Florida. As I said before, I don't love flying, but I was determined - and still am - not to let that fear grow in my kids. I was really nervous about traveling alone with a toddler; I had no idea how it would go. Who would watch her if I needed to pee? How would we get through security? How would I keep her entertained during the flight?

Once we got through security, which was actually pretty easy, we went to the gift shop to keep her occupied while we waited to board. I noticed a friend of mine was there shopping! I couldn't believe it! She and her husband were on our flight! I was glad I would have an ally on my flight. We went to the gate and sat down, and I tried to get Molly to eat some pizza before we boarded. I heard someone say, "Hi Mary!" I looked up, and there was another friend, a woman from my Bible study! She and her husband were on my flight, too! This was unreal to me! I knew two people on this flight! We got on the flight and sat down in our seats. Neither of my friends was within eyesight, but I knew they were there if I needed them. I looked to my right and saw a little girl in the next aisle. I recognized her as a cousin to the kids I used to nanny when I was in college. There was another person on my flight that I knew. I looked at the lady sitting directly next to me and realized she looked very familiar to me too. I had never talked to her in person, but I was pretty sure I knew who she was. "Are you Janet?" I asked. "Yes?" she said. I responded, "I am Mary Piasecki; we have been emailing back and forth about the meal train!" This lady Janet who was in my very row on this flight is the coordinator for the meal service at one of our church locations, and I had emailed, called, and texted her several times about providing meals for families at church! She has many grandchildren and joyfully helped me take care of Molly on the flight and even watched her when I went to the bathroom! And lastly, directly in the seat in front of me was a man who also attended my church, and his daughter was in my Bible study as well. I was literally surrounded by people ready and willing to help me on this flight! Each and every one of my concerns was addressed! I believe the Lord had his hand in that situation; I believe He orchestrated all of it and showed me just how good He is, above and beyond what I could've expected.

The flight overall was not bad. Molly did great, and it was pretty smooth. At the airport in Florida, we found Philip's aunt and got back to her house. It was late and I was tired, so I set Molly's bed up and got us ready for bed. Molly was not happy about sleeping somewhere she was not familiar with, and it took her over an hour to fall asleep.

On our second night in Florida, Molly still had not grown accustomed to the room she was staying in and was fighting bedtime. I was in my room texting Philip; Molly was quiet, so I assumed she had fallen asleep. Out of nowhere, Molly walked into my room. If you have never been in this situation, let me tell you, it is extremely alarming when you didn't know that your child had the ability to climb out of her crib and open doors, and suddenly she appears next to you - it is scary. Now I had a huge problem - what to do with her? She can open every door in the house and can climb out of her crib. I was not able to keep her contained. I started texting a couple of my mom friends, asking them for advice. Their advice was the same and simple - be consistent. One of them threatened to disown me if I gave in to her. Thus began one of the longest hours of my parenting career. I would put her in her crib; she would cry and say, "No!" I would walk out. She would climb out, open the door, and come get me. I would pick her up and put her back in. She would climb out and come to me. I would put her back in. Each time she would scream and cry, "No no no;" it was heartbreaking, but what was I to do? She does not sleep in the same bed as me. She talks and laughs and hits my face and stays up way past her bedtime, so neither of us would get any sleep if I tried that. I repeated this over and over and over for about an hour, and finally she gave up and went to sleep. This repeated itself for each nap and each bedtime for the remainder of the trip. Though each time was shorter and shorter.

We had a lot of fun in Florida. Molly loved swimming and going out to eat. We went on walks and just relaxed. I had just learned that Baby Boy was a boy and was very much into finding a name for him. I went through many, many baby name lists and downloaded several baby name apps. I found a few I liked and sent them to Philip while he was away. I found one on an app that I absolutely loved and adored. Ander. Sort of like Andrew but more unique, but not so unique that people think it is super weird. I immediately fell in love with it. I sent Philip a picture of Molly in the tub with bathtub toy letters that read "MOLLY ANDER" in the background, so he knew I was serious about liking that name. We tried to talk to Daddy as much as we could while we were gone. But he was super busy and the time difference made things difficult, but we did our best; and thankfully, the time went by fast in the best way possible.

Our flight back home was not full of as many familiar people, but we still knew a few. Molly did really well as long as I fed her a steady stream of snacks. After the plane landed, I set her back on her own seat for a minute, but didn't buckle her in. A second later, we turned into our gate to park, and Molly flew off the seat. She was fine, but I was mortified. The man who was sitting next to me the whole flight looked at me and said, "You're a really good mom!" WHAT A NICE MAN. Even though he had just seen my kid go flying (Okay, that is dramatic; she gracefully floated to the airplane floor.), he had noticed my actions before that and took the time to assure me I was still a good mom. Take note, reader, being nice isn't always time-consuming or hard, and it can go a long way.

My mom picked us up from the airport and dropped us off at home. It was around 10 p.m. when we got home, and Philip was in the air on his way home from the wedding. I got a text from a doula client that she was in labor. This was the only night I didn't have built-in coverage, as Philip was still gone. I'd thought the odds were slim that she would go into labor that night. Babies have their own timeline, and since the baby was coming, I had to go. I drove down to a friend's house and dropped Molly off. I apologized because I had no idea how she was going to do because she'd slept so horribly in Florida.

I got to the hospital as Philip landed in London and checked in to see how we were doing at home. I told him I was over an hour away from home and at a hospital with a client! The birth was incredible, mama was a rockstar, and before Philip had even boarded his flight to the States - mom was pushing! I left the hospital a couple of hours later, exhausted but feeling so alive at the same time. I love birth and watching mamas give birth. I just love being there to help in any way I can. Philip was arriving in Detroit the next afternoon. I was so tired from the travel and staying up late at the hospital, but I decided I couldn't wait one more second to see him and made a plan to surprise him at the airport! It was so fun, and he could not believe that we drove all that way to see him. Even though it was well over a year ago, Molly still looks at the picture from that day and says, "That was when we were at the airport for Daddy!"

Chapter 12

On Easter we left on a family trip to Italy. My husband's family and our little family unit of three spent two weeks in Europe together. As I have mentioned, I am not extremely easy-going. I tend to be high stress, and I do not do well under not a lot of sleep. This trip worried me because of all the flights and time changes. To my surprise, the long flight from Detroit went better than I'd hoped. Molly only slept an hour or two, though. And I did not sleep at all. I continually got more and more stressed out that she wasn't sleeping, which stopped me from sleeping. From Detroit, we flew to Germany and then to Florence. The flight from Germany to Florence was only 1.5 hours long. I finally got Molly to fall asleep on my lap. Since Molly was settled in, Philip moved to an empty seat on the other side of the plane to look at the beautiful view of the Swiss Alps down below. Then without warning, Molly sat up, coughed, and threw up on me. Multiple times. I didn't know if it was motion sickness or the flu, and I didn't know which one I wanted it to be. She was scared and exhausted, and I did not know what to do. My shirt was covered in vomit. She was terrified because she had never thrown up before. She just laid her head on my shoulder, and I tried to stay calm and not cry. Everyone around us moved because a child was throwing up. Philip and his parents sprang into action. Finding spare clothes and anything in the diaper bag that would help Molly.

When we landed, I was not at all excited about being in Italy. I was worried about my daughter. I saw an airport medic's office and took her in. The language barrier was bigger than I was expecting it to be. He knew no English, and I knew no Italian other than "pizza." He took her temperature and rattled off a number in Italian while showing me a thermometer reading in Celsius. I don't know anything about the metric system, so I did not know what that meant. I sat her on the bed, and he brought over an IV pole. At this point I realized we were not going to be able to communicate, so I picked her up and left. I was hoping she had maybe the stomach flu or maybe motion sickness. I did not know which one would be worse. When we got her in the car to go to the hotel, she threw up again in my hands.

Over the next three days it became painfully clear that Molly had the stomach flu. She threw up a couple of more times and got a really bad diaper rash a couple of days later. She had a low grade fever, and I was really glad I had packed my thermometer. I stayed in our condo for 24 hours straight with her. I was texting my mom, and she was trying to give advice and encouragement. All I wanted was to be home and with my mom. I felt like a little kid again, but the reality was that I wasn't a little kid. I had a little kid to take care of, whether I wanted to or not. It was really hard and really scary. She was in pain every time she went to the bathroom, and every time she went to the bathroom we had to change her, which meant more pain. It was terrible, and I sobbed on multiple occasions. I envisioned us having to take her to the hospital to get fluids and them having to stick her with an IV. But there was this added layer of a language barrier. I think it is vital to be able to communicate very clearly with doctors and nurses, and I was panicking thinking of not being able to do so.

Thankfully we didn't end up needing to go to the hospital. Within the first week, Molly slowly got back to her normal self. I decided to try to make the most out of the trip since we were in freakin' Europe. We took some day trips to different cities around Italy. We went to Florence and ate food and looked at the sights. It was a fun day, until we got in the car and she threw up again. That was the last time she threw up though. Even though I basically feared her throwing up the entire rest of the trip, I did my best to let my guard down and enjoy it. It is funny all the things you hear about Italy that are actually true. Everywhere we went all the old Italian women would come up to Molly and, literally, pinch her cheeks. Then they would tell us how beautiful and brilliant she is. They also just went on and on about how beautiful I am, I was just glowing, and she got her good looks from me. Or something similar to that. I was going off of facial expressions. I know a decent amount of Sign Language and so, as I tried to read their body language and gestures, that is about the closest thing I could come up with, but I think it is spot on.

While we were in Italy, Philip and I took a babymoon to Germany to visit my cousins who live there. We figured we may never be in Europe again, so we may as well take advantage of it. With Molly being sick, it definitely made me nervous to leave her, but thankfully she was pretty much back to normal by the time we left. We were gone a total of 2 nights but did not see her for almost 4 full days. To date that was the longest I had ever been away from her. Philip and I set out on our journey through Europe alone. We were going to take the train from Loro Ciuffenna to Pisa, and then fly to Frankfurt. Philip and I were on the train just taking it all in. The Italian people were INSISTENT that I must not stand (as I was 25 weeks pregnant but I looked almost full-term), and so I found myself sitting across from a kind Italian woman. She asked me where we were going, or maybe I asked her a question, I am not sure which. How it started is beside the point. She started telling me that we were in fact NOT on the right train and this train would never take us to Pisa. She told us we must get off at the next stop and get on another train. Philip told me he was sure we were on the right one. But this native woman was telling me we were getting ourselves lost. She must know! Our phones are not accurate; OLD ITALIAN WOMEN ARE NEVER WRONG. Philip and I went back and forth a few times, but ultimately Philip told me he would follow me. So we got off at the next stop and followed her to another train and got on it. When it started moving, we were instantly going in the wrong direction completely. I panicked. We got off and on trains and tried to ask questions, but no one knew what I was trying to say. And using American Sign Language is not helpful in the least to people who probably don't know Italian Sign Language. So I gave up all hope of getting to Germany. I told Philip we needed to call his family to come pick us up. He looked at the maps one more time and found the right train. We got on it and somehow it dropped us off at the airport in Pisa. Now, would I say I was wrong in following that woman? Yes. Yes, I would. In fact, I wonder if sometimes she still thinks about the American couple she decided to lie to and get completely lost on purpose and laughs to herself. I wonder if that year at Christmas she gathered her family around the table and told the story of the gullible pregnant American and her doting husband who followed her every word. I wonder if her eyes fill with tears as she tells her family, "I just pointed to a random train! AND THEY GOT ON IT! HAHAHA!" Or maybe it was a complete accident. Who is to say?

When we got back from Germany and first saw Molly, our reunion was honestly precious. She saw me and yelled, "MAMA! MAMA!" Our whole ride back to the condo she hugged my head and kept touching my face, like she couldn't believe I was real. I really enjoyed getting away with Philip for a couple of days; he is my best friend, and I have so much fun with him. But oh, seeing Molly again was one of the best memories of that trip.

We flew back home a few days later, and the flight was fine. Minus the super bumpy landing and the exhaustion. I am not a great traveler, but I can say that I did it. I took a toddler to Europe whilst pregnant, mixed with the stomach flu, and I lived to tell the tale. Philip and I remember this part differently, but I remember one particular day when Molly was sick and I was miserable, he told me I could name the baby whatever I wanted. He has no memory of this, and I suppose it could have been a dream, but this is where I solidified in my mind that the baby would be named Ander.

Chapter 13

THE END OF ANDER'S PREGNANCY

Philip and I were waffling back and forth on what the name of our son would be. I was pretty much positive I wanted Ander to be the name. Philip was too, but we just were not committed. We finally decided on Ander Philip Piasecki. Once we were sure, I ordered a blanket with his name on it. Once you invest $20 on a custom blanket, you can't go back. Philip had to go on a work trip to Ohio, and while he was gone the blanket came in. Seeing his name in writing made me cry and I knew that I knew that I knew that was his name.

We tried to keep the name a secret from everyone. We didn't want people's opinions, and we just wanted to save something for ourselves. It slowly got leaked to a couple of people but ultimately, I am proud to say, we managed to keep it mostly unknown. We told Molly the name, but she couldn't say it properly. She insisted on calling him "Brother" or "894." Where "894" came from, we will never know; but anyone who asked her brother's name got that response. A friend of mine thought it meant Ander would come on August 9th at 4:00AM (8/9, 4:00). Even though he was due on July 20th, that seemed out of control crazy and was never going to happen.

The summer of 2018 was really hot. Like blazing hot. I had never been pregnant in the summer before, and I did not plan this pregnancy around the summer heat. I went through most of the summer being larger than a whale. Every year for our anniversary Philip and I go to a Tigers baseball game. This year must have been some sort of record high. We bought tickets that were nice and close to the field, but they were in direct sunlight. I spent most of the game in the shade, drinking water, then subsequently going to the bathroom, and eating ice cream. I felt really bad because we had splurged for close seats and did not even end up sitting in them - but I was melting into a pool of pregnancy sweat.

I have an amazing friend named Alicia and she offered to come and clean my house, because I was feeling overwhelmed and I was big. I said no many times before I finally said yes. And she came and scrubbed my bathroom from top to bottom! She came back the next week with our friend Sarah, and they cleaned my basement storage room. If you don't have friends in your life like Alicia and Sarah - I pray you find some. I've said it before and I will say it again - having good people around you is basically crucial to this parenthood thing. Nay, it is crucial to this life thing. If you don't have amazing people in your life, ask God for them. I did and now I have a circle of incredible people around me, constantly supporting me.

As I approached my due date, people started the questions. If you've ever had a baby, you know the questions. "Are there twins in there?" "Can you even get bigger?" "Are you SURE there's only one?" I stopped going to church for a couple of weeks because I just couldn't handle it. But I still had to go out in public. The cashier at Sam's told me she was SURE there were twins in there - and she is never wrong about these things. Well, Helen, there is a first time for everything. Philip and I went to the movies, and he told a man I would stab him if he didn't stop asking me if I was having twins. Joanna Gaines had her baby boy, so now I wasn't even pregnant when she was. What was the point of going on?

My due date came and went. I had hoped I would go before my due date. With Molly I had gone 41 weeks and 5 days. I did not think it would be possible to go longer than that. Pregnancies get shorter not longer. Right?

The End of Ander's Pregnancy

I mean, this is what they tell us! RIGHT?!?! Someone, please tell me this is how it is supposed to go.

Even all of my neighbors joined in on Bump Watch 2018. "Any day now, huh?" They would say as I waddled by their houses. I imagine they all hung out day and night waiting to see me come huffing and puffing, trying to keep up with my toddler (who had either become extremely fast or I was becoming extremely slow). "George! George! Here she comes again! Yes, George, she is still pregnant. No, George, I don't think she can get any bigger! We should call the papers and have them write a story on her!" Or something to that effect.

I lived on watermelon, strawberries, and ice cream. With each passing day, we were just so sure that I was going to give birth, so we would go get ice cream to celebrate. I would go to bed thinking surely I would wake up in the middle of the night with a contraction. Sometimes I did, but I always woke up in the morning still pregnant. Contractions started and stopped several times. I had not had this with Molly. That time, when contractions started, they did not stop.

As I mentioned, I was still working out through most of my pregnancy, but once I reached 40 weeks Jill noticed that Ander's head wasn't quite centered in my pelvis. She sent me to a chiropractor for an adjustment, and a couple of days later his head was centered and he sank lower. Together Jill and my chiropractor convinced me to stop working out and just walk and swim. They said it was better for my alignment. It was hot and our gym doesn't have A/C, so I agreed. After that, I grew an exponential amount. I could never get comfortable because I was enormous, I had heartburn, and I was burning up in the inferno that was late July in Michigan. I tried to be happy, I really did. I tried to soak up all the moments of it just being Molly, Philip, and I; but I just wanted to give birth.

I took to Facebook to keep some comic relief going. I asked people for suggestions on wide comfy sandals. I posted end of pregnancy memes and talked about how much I wanted to have this baby. I posted the lyrics of worship songs that were keeping me going. On July 23rd, three days past my due date, I posted a status and a friend commented that 8/8/18 was her guess. I said if I was still pregnant by then, I would need to be committed to a mental hospital.

July turned into August, and I was still pregnant. I was officially pregnant the same amount of time as with Molly. Then another week passed. I was 42 weeks pregnant. We started to be on a time crunch. Forty-three weeks was as comfortable as Philip, Jill, and I felt we could go without getting an induction. Jill didn't think I could find anyone to induce me because VBACS are scary and I had been pregnant for so long. I had taken a gamble on having a home birth, and it looked like I was losing. So I was headed for a C-section if I didn't go into labor by that Saturday.

On August 7th, 18 days past my due date, I was desperate to have this baby. My sister Laura suggested going to get acupuncture. I figured it couldn't hurt, so I agreed to try. She got me in contact with her acupuncturist, and I called her up and explained my situation. Once she heard I was so overdue, she told me she could fit me in that day but told me I needed to bring someone with me because she's had many people have their water break at her office. I drove an hour to her office and Laura met me there. I had never had acupuncture before, and I had zero idea what to expect. The acupuncturist put these little needles into key points on my body. Two in the small of my back and I laid on them, some in my legs, arms and fingers; then she hooked the needles up to an electric current. This was the weirdest part. The current made my hands twitch uncontrollably, and the needles in my back were not exactly comfortable. Nevertheless, I laid there for an hour and to my surprise, I began having contractions! I'd had contractions for several weeks, but these were longer and sort of bordering on painful. After the hour was up she unhooked me, and her assistant "milked" my legs, which basically means she massaged them and it was supposed to push something... into something... to make something happen, and I would go into labor. After that, the doctor came back in and - without warning, and I mean, not even a small heads up - put her hands a few inches from my head and chest while I laid on the table and began to call Mother Earth to bring forth this child. I don't remember her exact words, because in that moment I began praying in my head. I believe spirits are REAL and calling on anything other than the Holy Spirit is dangerous and real and not okay with me. I started rebuking her request and asking for protection over my heart! So, friends, word to the wise, maybe ask before you start praying or calling on things for people, because it can surely freak someone out.

Anywho, after all of that, it was time to drive home. When I left, all of the contractions stopped. In fact, I think this was the least amount of contractions I had felt in a while. I got home, and Philip and I started making peace with the upcoming C-section. I was going to get a pedicure and manicure and maybe even a blowout, and then go in, have a baby, and be on my way. It honestly didn't sound all that bad. I put Molly to bed and came out of her room to realize Philip had drawn me a bath, lit some candles, and poured me a glass of wine. (A small glass. It's fine, people.) So I took a bath, drank the wine, and went to bed. Knowing no matter what happened, it was going to be okay because I couldn't be pregnant forever.

Chapter 14

ANDER'S BIRTH

August 8th, 2018, 5:30 AM. I felt something like a tiny little elbow hitting me in my crotch and then like I had peed myself. I got up to go to the bathroom, and my unders were wet and there was some other stuff in it. I could not believe it!!! MY WATER BROKE! (Well, just a small part of it - the water breaks later on in this story and you don't want to miss it).

I called Jill to tell her and we both celebrated; she prayed for me, and I went back to bed. Or at least I tried. I texted my doula and my friends who were coming to the birth and then tried to go back to sleep. But that was almost impossible; I was so excited, and contractions had already started to pick up.

Around 7:30 contractions were getting to where I couldn't ignore them anymore. By 8:00 AM I started to think that this was starting to get going. I began to ask my birth team to come over. I had planned on having Molly with me at the birth, but I soon realized that wasn't really an option. I was breathing heavily and loudly during contractions, and Molly started mimicking me. I didn't want her to witness the intensity of emotions that was going to come. Philip called my mother-in-law to come get Molly. I had envisioned my birth a dozen times and a dozen different ways, with and without Molly there. I thought I would be extremely emotional saying goodbye to my baby for the last time before I had another baby, but saying goodbye to Molly was not at all emotional for me. Probably because I was in the middle of a contraction and it was all I could do to stay calm, let alone think about the significance of the moment. So I kissed her goodbye and switched back into labor mode.

For the rest of the story, I don't really remember the exact times. I just remember some blurry details and my thoughts surrounding them. I labored in my tub for a while with just Philip in the bathroom with me. Soon my doula came and walked me through several contractions. I was actually handling them better than I'd anticipated, which scared me.

Almost immediately, doubt settled into my head. These contractions were much more manageable than last time. I was talking and laughing in between them. One sign that many midwives, doulas, doctors, nurses look for is when mom stops talking between contractions. That is when you know this is serious business. The contractions I was having were strong, but I could get through them and back to reality quickly; so I panicked. "This can't be active labor then, can it?" "Well, if this isn't active labor, how much stronger are these going to get? I can't do this for 40 hours!" I had pictured this birth in my head a thousand times. It was going to be peaceful. I wanted it to be fast. Well, I don't know if anyone has ever told you that birth is 80% mental, but I can attest to you, that seems like truth.

Some of my doubts and fears I voiced, and some I held inside. My inner dialogue was a continual running of doubt and empowerment. Fear and prayers. Around and around.

I got out of the tub, and I labored on the couch. Philip would rub my arm or head during a contraction, and I could get through them. I was doing great for a while.

As Ander moved lower in my pelvis, I started to have to push. I pushed off and on and then... it happened. I pooped. I felt it happen. And I didn't care. From then on, I would walk around my house laboring in whatever room felt good at the time, and I would think, "Oh, I think I might be pooping," and then someone would wipe my butt. That is love. That is labor.

Then I started to freak out. I had prepared myself for all of the uterine contractions, but I didn't expect my butt to cramp up or the feeling of my hips separating. I hadn't thought about that, and it threw me.

I started spiraling again.

I was in the living room standing on a stool talking and laughing when someone said they could see his head. Jill and Tristany started gloving up. Someone rolled up the rug, and I was about to have a baby in my living room. But then I thought, "I can't almost be done. This is TOO EASY. I have to have hours left of this." They said as I was having these thoughts in my head, they could see my body close up, and Ander went back inside my body. At this point, my doula called Philip and me into our room for a regroup session. I laid down and tried to get my mind right. It worked for a while. I got through several contractions, and then a new sensation would hit and my body would clamp up and I would yell out, "I can't do this!!" or "Take me to the hospital; I want an epidural!" My whole team would tell me I could do this, I was doing this, if I went to the hospital I would just get a c-section. Eventually, I thought a c-section would be better than this. "I WILL TAKE MYSELF TO THE HOSPITAL!" And at another point, I really thought death would be better. After a while, I realized no one would take me to the hospital, so I didn't have a choice but to stay put.

Then I was lying on my bed pushing, and my water broke. No, no. My water EXPLODED in a great cloud of water. All over. It was a sight to behold. My midwife handled it like a champ - "Wasn't in my mouth this time" - and kept going, guiding me through labor.

I cried a lot between contractions. When he didn't just flop out onto the floor, I would instantly think, "I have hours left of this," and, "This hurts."

There was so much more pressure than I thought there would be. There started to not be any relief between contractions, and I would spiral even more. And then I would be so mad at myself. This was supposed to be peaceful. I was supposed to rock this and be in control, and I was reeling. I was sobbing. I was swearing. I was failing. I wanted him out of me.

I looked at each person on my birth team and asked them to let me give up. They all said no. My doula or midwife would suggest a position change, and I would outright refuse. I can't. I can NOT do that! I can't do this! I can NOT DO THIS ANYMORE! And everyone would say, "Yes, you can! You ARE!" and I would make it through another contraction. And on and on. I did ask Alexa to play "Champion" by Carrie Underwood, and that got me through for a while. Because I was made for this!!

For the grand finale, I was on my bed with 5 other people helping me. I labored leaning against a ball, on my side, kneeling, lunging. I would say, "You have no choice!" and move and keep going. I will spare you the gory details - I will say I was the opposite of glamorous when he was coming out. WOWZA. But my husband was behind me, breathing with me through pushes. People were saying, "He is so close! We can see his head!" and I would say, "Then pull him out!" Sometimes I would have a pep talk and get through contractions, but mainly I was crying and wanting it to be over. Someone said, "Just treat this like the hardest workout you have ever done!" and then I would push and I would think, "All you have and then some."

In between every contraction, my midwife would check his heart rate, and every single time he was handling them well. I knew my baby was okay. I knew this was going to end. I was just scared that it wouldn't. So on we pushed.

Everyone would get excited, and I could tell he was coming more. At one point someone said, "His whole head is out! Do you want to see?" "NO, I

WANT HIM OUT!!" Then the next thing I knew, Philip put him on my chest. And I just looked at this HUGE, beautiful baby! My baby! I started talking to him, and he coughed and then cried! He was okay! He was perfect! And then it hit me.

I did it. I got my VBAC. I got my home birth. And then the absolute flood of emotions. Part of me is sort of embarrassed, but most of me isn't. I started proclaiming how good God is. How He is so real, He is SO good! He helped me through this! He was so real and so good! And I did it, I pushed a baby out of me!! And then came the body-shaking sobs!

We got to spend time just Philip, Ander, and myself. We called our parents and told them it was over. Molly saw her brother over FaceTime, and she was so excited! It was pure bliss for hours. It was everything I could have wanted and then some.

He was measured and weighed (14-inch head, 15-inch chest, 22 inches long, 9lb 2oz), and then I was even more proud of myself. Dang, girl; dat's a big baby.

I want to take a minute and say home birth can be safe for low-risk women. Finding a midwife who is experienced and professional is the key to this. I do not regret my choice, and I would do it all again for Ander.

Chapter 15

AFTER ANDER'S BIRTH

Jill noticed my blood pressure wasn't where she wanted it to be. I hadn't been able to pee for a long time, and she tried to have me get up and go to the bathroom, but when I sat up, I almost passed out. My hearing got muffled, and my vision started to tunnel. I was looking at Jill square in the eye and said, "I think I am passing out, Jill!" She calmly talked to me, and I stayed with her and was able to stay awake. She pulled out her bag of tricks and started trying to get my blood pressure back up. She gave me a shot of Pitocin; I had two doses of a tincture that helps stop bleeding. We elevated my legs, I tried to drink fluids, all of it. But she didn't like that my blood pressure was not coming back up. She even had a full-body pressure cuff that she put on me. It was supposed to squeeze all the blood in my body to my head and I was immediately going to feel better. When she put it on, I didn't notice any difference at all. This is when Jill knew I was bleeding somewhere. We knew I had torn a little on the outside, but she was then sure I was bleeding inside. It was something she was familiar with, had seen before, and knew it was outside of her skill set. She had been tracking my blood loss and knew it was time to transfer me to the hospital.

The entire time she was doing all of her tricks and talking to me, she remained completely calm and professional. I never even knew there was an issue. She took her assistant into the hallway and came back in and said it was time to go to the hospital to get stitches and some fluids. I added I really wanted a catheter so I could empty my bladder. I was slightly concerned, but I wasn't ever scared. So they called 9-1-1, and an ambulance came. I was completely and totally with it. I grabbed my phone and texted my friend and neighbor, "Hey, don't panic. I have to go to the hospital because I'm so dehydrated. I'm going to get fluids. But please pray. I am typing this myself. So I'm ok." She responded that she had heard the ambulance and was worried but was praying and asked if I needed anything. I said I only needed prayer because I was getting anxious.

When you call 9-1-1 a billion people get dispatched. The first people to show up were two police officers. They got called to a house where there was a homebirth and the mom was bleeding. Maybe they thought they were going to see a crazy hippie with incense burning, chewing on her placenta with armpit hair blowing in the wind, or a woman who was nearly dead from blood loss and any of the NUMEROUS imminent complications that come with having a baby outside of a hospital. I am not sure what they were expecting, but I do not think they were expecting me. Let me set the scene: they came in, and I was lying on my bed, eating ice cream. Butt naked, with my hair a complete mess. Wearing a body glove, and there was birth aftermath everywhere. I think my placenta was sitting in a bowl on the nightstand. Okay, do you have a rough picture of what these two cops walked in to see? Good, let's keep going. I was still on an absolute high from having a natural birth. They asked me what was up. I smiled a huge smile and said, "I JUST HAD A 9LB 2OZ BABY! Right here! ON THIS BED! But I am fine; I need some fluids and probably some stitches but - home birth is safe! It's okay!"

They laughed. They laughed. Just remember that. We were all laughing and joking.

I apologized because I get chatty when I am nervous. Then the paramedics got there. A guy and a girl. The girl casually walked in and asked me what was going on. I proudly exclaimed I had just had a 9LB 2OZ baby, right here, on my bed, and I probably needed some fluids. If you've ever had a natural birth, you may know that there can be a wave of absolute euphoria that comes over you. I hadn't had a single drug, and I was on cloud 9; I was also beaming with pride that I'd had a VBAC. I started telling the paramedics that they were doing amazing jobs. They had truly found their calling, and they were amazing at their jobs. The guy, whose name I do not remember, told me it was his first day on the job. And I just couldn't handle that. I was so proud of him for getting that job and couldn't believe he got called to MY birth and that he was there to help ME! So much pride for this man I had never seen before.

I don't know the specifics, but apparently it was out of their scope of work to hook me up to an IV, so they had to call in another guy to come and hook me up to an IV. He was a police officer and a medic. So we casually waited around for him to come, and when he came, I gladly filled him in on my accomplishments.

They got me onto a stretcher and started wheeling me out into the living room. The new paramedic accidentally bumped into the coffee table, which knocked over a picture and broke the frame. I quickly told him that it was okay, don't let that deter you from YOUR CALLING! You are doing a great job!

While I was being loaded into the ambulance, my husband was packing up our hours-old son into the car seat to drive to the hospital to see his wife that, yet again, had ended up being hospitalized. He never once let on that he was scared, but I found out later he was very nervous.

In the ambulance, the medic and I chatted. I asked him multiple times if he thought I was dying. He always said, "No! The lights aren't even on, you are going to be fine!" He said he had heard I did CrossFit, and I was all too eager to tell him all.about.it. He thought that part of the reason I had been able to stay alert was because I had been in such great shape. If I hadn't already been incredibly proud of myself, I became beyond proud of myself for working out my whole pregnancy. I asked him if he was a cop or a paramedic. He said he was both. I was so impressed! I mean it was like he was my own son! Two jobs! Two skillsets! Those after birth motherly hormones are REAL. We knew someone in common and chatted about him for a minute. He called ahead to the ER and told them I was coming in. We got to the hospital, and they wheeled me into the ER. You would have thought I was in the Thanksgiving Day parade! I was waving and smiling at everyone. "I just had a baby!!! At home!!" I got wheeled into my ER Room, and it all changed.

I was in a tiny room full of easily 6-10 people. Jill was with me, and I could hear her explaining to them what to look for, but they ignored her. I heard her saying, "This is a trickle bleed; it will probably be in the upper back part of her vagina." But soon her calm voice was drowned out by doctors yelling. One doctor asked me if I consented to have human blood and human plasma. I was confused, because just minutes ago I was on cloud nine and having a leisurely chat with the paramedic. Now the doctor was asking if I wanted to have a blood transfusion. I knew I had lost a decent amount of blood and I was here to check for a bleed, so I said, "..If I need it." "YOU DO! Get the blood and hang it wide open STAT!" Then one of the doctors asked me if I consented to a vaginal check; she said she needed to see if I had parts of my placenta still inside. I said okay. Then she proceeded to shove both hands nearly up to her elbows inside of me and pulled out all she could get her hands on. I screamed! The pain was worse than labor! I grabbed the hand of the nurse next to me. "Sorry!" I said. "It is okay; you squeeze as hard as you need to!" he replied. The doctors asked me about my placenta.

"Where is your placenta? Did all of it come out?
"It's at my house! Maybe in the garbage? It all came out - I know it did."
"You think it did, but it's easy to think that! Make sure it's all out!"
"I know it did; Jill told me it was all out!"

More hands inside of me.

"OW!! OH MY GOD, HELP ME!"
"We need to stop this bleeding! We need a bag of Pitocin!"
"I already had a Pitocin shot!"
"It doesn't matter- we need more. Someone go up to L&D STAT!"

People were running in and out of the room. The blood came from the blood bank and was hung. The nurses remained calm, and doctors barked orders and threw questions at me. I told them I had not emptied my bladder in hours and asked if I could get a catheter and maybe that could help them find the source of the bleed and I could get some relief. They asked what was around me. At some point, Jill came back into the room and explained to them what it was. A body glove to direct blood to my head. They all but laughed in her face. I heard them mocking it in the operating room later. She told them they needed to take it off slowly, but they didn't listen. They took it off and saw my c-section scar. I hadn't planned on telling them I was a VBAC. It didn't seem to matter. Once they saw that, they ordered an ultrasound STAT! They needed to check for rupture.

I asked if I was going to be okay. I don't know why I kept looking for reassurance, but they were just so frantic; I thought surely they would have calmed down by now and realized I was okay. The doctor said when I came in I was as white as a sheet and they definitely thought I was going to die. "The nurses told me I was going to be okay!" "Yeah, you lost over half of your blood volume; I thought you were a goner." Panic tried to set in again, because she had either lied at first or was lying now. Was I ever going to be okay?

During this time with everyone yelling and calling out orders, I started to panic. They were not calm, and they did not hide it. I asked the nurses if they thought I was going to die; they all assured me I wasn't. But the doctors were frantic. The ER doctors made me fully believe I was about to die. I was a 29-year-old woman about to leave her 2 kids without a mom and husband a widower. I remember lying back and looking at the clock on the wall behind me. 23:28; I noted the time. I'd seen a lot of hospital shows and started to wonder how soon they were going to call time of death while they were looking at that clock. I started to think in just a few moments I was going to see Jesus face to face for the first time. I would get to see my dad and Tommy; that thought comforted me. But my kids would be without a mom, and Philip would be a young widower. I wondered if he would be able to find donor milk for Ander or if he would need formula. I hoped Molly would remember me and hoped she would understand that I loved her and I wished I got to see her grow up. I started to feel at peace about dying, which made me believe it was imminent. I know when you die you feel a sense of peace, so I figured this was God preparing me to die at any moment.

Then suddenly a doctor came in and asked me if they could examine Ander. I snapped completely out of my thought process.

"What? Why? Is he okay?" I asked.
"I can't guarantee that until we see him."
"Well, did something happen to him?"
"We don't know; we just want to look at him. Your plan wasn't to come to the hospital, but your plan changed, so I think we need to look at him."
"Okay; yes, that's fine." I mean she had told me that Ander wasn't okay, right? That something happened to him between me having him and getting here, that is what she told me. I think.

Then Philip and Jill came into the room. They said Ander was fine and there was no reason for him to be looked at or admitted. The doctor stuck by my bed and told me he had a bruise on his head and needed Vitamin K. My heart dropped; okay, if that's what he needs, then yes. Let's do it! Jill said she had vitamin K for him. "Drops aren't enough; he needs the shot!" "I have the shot in my medical bag!" I didn't know it, but out in the hallway while I was making my peace with the Lord about dying, Jill and Philip were being berated by this doctor for thinking that having a baby at home was safe. The doctor said we were irresponsible for doing this and Jill was endangering women and should never do it again. The doctor tried to get Philip to have Ander admitted for observation, and when he said no, she came into my room to try and get me to comply.

Philip made them leave the room. The doctor didn't want to leave. She said she was fine with doing things naturally, but the baby needed to be examined. Philip again told her she needed to leave. Philip and Jill told me all about their conversations with the doctor. Jill told me Ander was fine; his bruise wasn't that big, and she would give him vitamin K herself. There was no need for these doctors to touch him. I had to decide at that moment who I trusted more. This doctor who was loudly and urgently telling me one thing about my baby, or this woman who had gently, calmly, compassionately, and wonderfully guided me and walked with me through my entire pregnancy and labor. A woman I knew, whom I had just completely trusted with my life and my son's. That was not going to change now under these circumstances. I chose Jill. I looked at Jill, and I told her I thought I was going to die and I was terrified of leaving my baby. She told me there was no way that was true. She logically explained to me that I hadn't lost that much blood and they were giving me more blood, so that wasn't on the table. I believed her, and I was calmed almost instantly. Jill left to give Ander vitamin K, and Philip stayed with me. The ultrasound tech came in and started giving me an ultrasound.

"Is this your first baby?"
"No, my second."
"Is this your second pregnancy?"
"Yes."
"So you have 3 kids?"
"No, just two."
"...Do you have twins?"

115

"No, a two-year-old and I just had a baby a few hours ago."

"Oh, you're not pregnant right now?"

"No!"

They had never told her what to look for. She thought she was doing an ultrasound on a pregnant mother. No one told her I had just given birth. She didn't know she was looking for a uterine rupture, placenta, or a bleed.

Philip left the room, and Jill came back in. They still couldn't find the bleed. A male doctor came in and started digging around my innermost parts with two hands. "FOR THE LOVE OF GOD, YOU HAVE TO STOP; THAT HURTS! I DO NOT CONSENT ANYMORE!!!!!! IF YOU DO THAT AGAIN, I NEED TO BE PUT UNDER!" Jill said, "You all heard her! Hands off!" From the hallway, Jill's assistant heard a nurse say to another nurse, "They're making an example out of her because she had a home birth. I had a home birth, but I would never tell them."

They wheeled me up to the surgical waiting area. I waited there with Philip for around an hour. Jill joined us and told me Ander was home safe with Tristany again. Thankfully she was still nursing her son, so she stayed with Ander and nursed him as needed throughout the night. I was so relieved that he was safe and didn't need formula. Over the radio sitting in the nurses' station, I heard a call come in for a patient with an arterial bleed. I was moved to the end of the line. Eventually, they took me to another floor to use the L&D operating room. As I was being wheeled into the OR, doctors came up to me and asked me where my placenta was. I told them probably in the garbage and I didn't have it with me. In the OR they took their time putting me under. Part of me was still afraid I wouldn't wake up, but the next thing I knew I was alone in recovery.

A nurse walked over and told me she was my nurse. I asked if I was okay. "Yeah, but I heard you almost bled out when you came in." "Did I have a tear?" "Yeah, a really deep one in the upper back part of your vagina. You bled a lot."

Wait. This is the exact thing that Jill said I had? This is something that is NOT unique to homebirth? This has nothing to do with a VBAC? This is because I pushed really hard and had a big baby? This could have happened in a hospital birth? Wait, my midwife caught this in time? Wait, wait, wait… we were responsible and came into the hospital and didn't shun the medical community like paranoid idiotic hippies?!?! That's what you're saying? I waited for my apology or acknowledgment that we were right. But it didn't come. In fact, the opposite happened. The story got around to everyone there that I came in white as a sheet, almost dead and bleeding out. Every nurse heard the story, and everyone thought they saved me from the brink of death.

The next morning Ander was brought to me. Tristany brought him up on her way to work. Soon after she left, Jill called Philip and told him I looked unrecognizable to Tristany. Philip had been with me the whole time and didn't notice as it was happening. But I was being pumped with so much fluid and blood and plasma, I had begun to swell. My eyes were almost swollen shut. I looked terrible. We told them we didn't want any more blood or plasma, but I was on my last dose. I was given a total of 8 blood and plasma bags. I fully believe this was more than I had lost, which was why I looked so terrible.

An OB doctor came in to do rounds. The instant I saw her, I recognized her. She was the Resident, now Attending, who had told me I could NEVER, EVER have a home birth when I had Molly. She asked me how I was feeling.

"I am feeling pretty good."
"Do you know why you're feeling good?"

"...Because I got some blood and got all stitched up?"

"NO. Because you're young and healthy. If you had been older or unhealthy, you would have died last night."

"If I were older or unhealthy, I wouldn't have had a home birth."

"You should never have attempted a homebirth! Especially after a c-section. You almost died!"

She went on to say how dumb we were. And Philip told her we were here to make sure I was okay and did not need to validate our choices to her. She asked why I didn't use the midwives their hospital had. I said because they didn't take VBACs. I said I loved their midwives, but I couldn't be a patient with them unless I wanted a scheduled c-section. She said she just wanted to make sure I was not going to tell my friends to have a home birth.

WELL, DR. NEGATIVE - HERE I AM, TELLING MY FRIENDS TO HAVE A HOMEBIRTH! If you have a trusted, certified, experienced midwife, and you are a low-risk mother, then it can be safe, and I 100% would recommend. I also believe you should have at least one ultrasound to check the position of the placenta and things like that. Jill required one, as well as blood work. She knows what she is doing.

Later that day we got moved to another floor where they wanted to keep me for another 24 hours. We definitely did not want to stay for 24 hours. We figured if they had done their job, I could go home, and if I needed something I would come back. While we were sitting there, our new nurse walked in. It was none other than NURSE JENNY. Nurse Jenny! The nurse from Molly's pregnancy! I couldn't believe it! We chatted and caught up. She was a mom now, and we talked about kids and our lives. I told her my side of the story and told her I wanted to leave. She said if I came in once for medical attention, she thought I would come in if I needed it. I said I wasn't afraid to leave AMA if I had to. She went and told the doctors I wanted to leave, and they said hospital policy was for me to stay 24 hours for observation. So Nurse Jenny went and got us AMA papers, and we left the hospital with our under 24-hour old baby.

When I was writing and editing this section, I went online and got my official medical records from this time. I wanted to fact-check myself and make sure I wasn't exaggerating. I was not. I even saw multiple times where they referred to Jill as a lay midwife. Which is not true. There are five kinds of midwives. Certified Nurse-Midwife (CNM), Certified Midwife (CM), Certified Professional Midwife (CPM), Direct-Entry Midwife (DEM), Lay Midwife. Direct-entry midwives participate in births at home and in free-standing birth centers. CNM, CM, and CPMs require training and schooling. They are held accountable to a board of people. No national certification or licensing is needed for direct-entry midwives, and each state has its own legal requirements for education and licensing. Lay midwife refers to an uncertified or unlicensed midwife who often has an informal education, such as apprenticeship or self-study, rather than a formal education. Jill is a CPM, and I believe they called her a lay midwife as an insult and to discredit her.

Chapter 16

POTTY TRAINING

So I had survived the summer with two kids and then it was fall. Molly started to become more and more aware of her bathroom habits, to the point that it made me uncomfortable to change her diaper. She would stand in the kitchen or living room and poop in her diaper; then she would walk up to one of us and say, "I pooped. Let's go change my diaper," then go to her room and get the wipes and try to help clean herself up. It was weird. We were over it. That was one factor, mixed with how much keeping two kids in diapers was surely going to bankrupt us. So we decided to potty train her again. Yes, again. I had tried to potty train her while I was pregnant, in an attempt to prepare her for having a baby brother. As soon as she turned 2, I decided I wanted to potty train her. I read the book Oh Crap Potty Training and felt like I was ready to teach her. The method is basically you take away diapers except for nap and bedtime; they walk around the house in the buff. Molly was just peeing all over the house. Left and right. You're supposed to stay calm and just direct them to the potty. She started holding in her pee and poop because she was terrified of the changes that potty training brings. She would even hold it in at night and keep her diaper dry, and then pee all over the floor upon waking up. By day FIVE of this, she was not catching on at all. She peed on the kitchen floor and excitedly exclaimed, "My peepee!!" I was so frustrated. She was not supposed to be happy that she was peeing all over - it was supposed to be a bad thing. I definitely was not patient or kind every time - or if I am honest, any of the time. I think I made her scared, and I think I made this experience terrible for her. We fought a lot those five days. Philip and I were miserable. Potty training will take all the confidence you have as a parent, break it down, throw it on the floor, and pee on it.

At some point during Potty Training Torture Week, we were giving Molly a bath. While she was in the tub she looked at me with terror in her eyes, and before we could process what her face was desperately trying to tell us and grab her out, she had pooped in the tub. She has only pooped once or twice in the tub in her life. I truly don't remember if this was the first or second time. But Philip and I looked at each other and said, "Yeah, so two kids is going to be enough for us." Though I knew in my heart of hearts I would change my mind and want another one. Moments like that, on top of potty training, made us question things. Such as the sanity of people who willingly have more than 2 kids - I do not understand how they go into potty training and poopy tubs, eyes wide open, three times.

On Friday of that week, I had had enough. Molly was tantruming, I was tantruming, I was not leaving the house, and I was squatting down every hour or so to wipe pee off the floor. I slapped a diaper on her and decided we were done potty training. MAYBE FOREVER...ASK ME IF I CARE!!! She could be in a diaper until she was 5 or 6 and it would not bother me one iota!

The next morning, I happily made myself a cup of coffee, and Molly - for the first time in her little life - asked me for a cup of "foffee". I poured her some milk in a mug, and she sat next to me at the kitchen table. She looked at how I held my cup and did her best to position her hands in the same way. Together we sat and drank our coffee. I could not believe it. Even though she was furious with me moments before, and after, she still loved me and wanted to be like me, be near me, and mimic me. She taught me a huge lesson that day. A lesson I sometimes struggle to implement. Just because I am mad at someone in the moment, it shouldn't - and doesn't - erase all the love, trust, and memories I have built up from before. I learned a lot that time around.

This second time I wanted to be more prepared, so I read the book Oh Crap Potty Training again. I couldn't start and then stop again, so once we started, this was it - our final shot. The first day, I told Molly, "You are not wearing a diaper anymore, so if you pee it will go on the floor." She didn't believe me, and a few minutes later she was standing at her play kitchen watching a stream of urine hit the floor. I picked her up and said, "Pee pee goes in the potty." By the time nap time rolled around, she was running to get to the potty! Philip and I could not believe it. It was just such a completely different experience than the first time. Week one was full of ups and downs. She definitely had accidents, but she was trying to get to the potty. I followed her around with a little potty seat all day. We put a diaper on her at nap and at bedtime, but she would wake up dry some of the time. Day 3 we hit a wall, and I think she realized we meant business. She would sob and say, "I do not want to use my potty!" Then kick her potty seat. How many more times can I say "potty"? Let's see.

We were persistent, and we were not going back on our potty training goal. I did break the OCPT Method and took her out in a Pull Up. I needed to get out of the house so we took her to AWANA, which is our midweek Children's Bible program at our church. It might be Molly's favorite place in the entire world. She wore a Pull Up with underwear under it. I wanted her to feel if she peed all over. When we got home, she was dry. She did great! I knew the first poop on the potty was going to be scary. She usually pooped standing up, and this was a whole new ball game. She would hold it and hold it as long as she could. I knew she was reaching her breaking point, so I took off her pants and had her walk around the house naked. I figured cleaning poop off the floor was better than cleaning it out of pants. I followed her around the house and waited. She asked if I could put shorts on her, and for a minute I considered it. She gave me that look that I know so well. It was coming, and this time she would not be able to hold it. I told her she could stand and I would hold the potty. She just cried and squeezed her cheeks even tighter. Then I had the idea that maybe she would want to see it come out. I don't know why I thought maybe it wouldn't scare her. It worked. She sat down on her potty and watched herself poop. Then the biggest party happened! She got to flush it down the toilet and we called the grandparents and aunts to tell them our exciting news! Our friend was coming to pick up his son from piano lessons during that time, so I did not hesitate to fill him in! I am such a cool mom.

At night we put her potty in her crib with her, and she loved it. She would sit and squeeze out any amount of pee she had in her and yell loudly, "I WENT PEE PEE!" After a few nights of having to maneuver her diaper, we put her in a Pull-Up so she could pull it up and down easier. Eventually, she took off the Pull-Up and still woke up dry. From then on, she has only worn a Pull-Up a handful of times. So yeah, Molly 100% night trained herself with a few accidents in the mix, but it was nothing I did. I can't really take pride in it, because I mostly messed up a lot along the way.

One time Molly got a yeast infection, probably due to her trying to wipe herself, and it was making her potty training derail. She started peeing everywhere all the time. I thought she was being rebellious, and I was not nice to her. I told her she could not wear her big girl underwear anymore, because she kept peeing in them. If she was going to keep peeing in her underwear, she wasn't a big girl, she was a baby. She was so heartbroken and hurt and mad at me. I was mad at myself but frustrated at her rebellion. I still think about that day from time to time. It was not that long ago really. I was so unkind to her, and I really hurt her feelings. After a few more accidents and tears, we took her to a few doctors and realized she had developed an infection.

By Halloween Molly was pretty much potty trained, and we took her and Ander trick or treating, but I put her in a Pull Up. She had a blast galloping around the neighborhood dressed as a unicorn. She was terrified of all the big kids in costumes and would stop on a dime and run the other way when she saw them. Halloween decorations, however, did not bother her a bit. She stood and pointed to each bulb and proudly called out the colors to us. "Green! Orange! Purple! Green! Orange! Purple!" Not to mention every house was giving her candy, and she was with her best friends! It's one of my favorite memories so far of having two kids! I think we lasted an hour, and by the end both kids were crying, so we headed home and discovered that she had stayed dry all evening. That Saturday we took her to one of her favorite stores, The Home Depot, and decided against a Pull-Up. To my surprise, she stayed dry the whole time. We didn't bring Pull-Ups to Thanksgiving at my brother's house. The only accident she had was when I didn't pull her pants all the way down and she peed on them. But that was my fault. Just like that, we had a potty-trained toddler. Now she is 3 years and a few months old and prefers to hold in her pee instead of stopping her playing, so she has accidents from time to time. But we did it, we potty trained her.

Chapter 17

WORST CASE SCENARIO

I mentioned before that when Molly was born I had postpartum anxiety. I have dealt with anxiety my entire life. But when Molly was born, it was something entirely different. I could not let anyone else hold her without picturing them dropping her. Every time I took her downstairs, I pictured myself tripping and falling down the stairs and Molly being hurdled through the air. I never wanted to go on a date with Philip because I would not be able to leave her with anyone. I trusted them, but I just wanted to be able to be there in case the unthinkable happened. It felt like I had more control over everything that way. Once we started doing CrossFit, that went away. All of my nervous energy got channeled into working out, and I was able to get my anxiety under control. I still had times of anxiety though.

So if Molly would fall or get hurt, I'd tell my husband all my fears were justified and if I weren't watching her, something bad would happen. This does not logically make sense, but Anxiety does not care. Anxiety wants to give you a false sense of control; it wants you to stay home and miss out on things because too many bad things can happen. Philip is the best at reassuring me when I need reassurance; he would always tell me, "If she were really hurt or broke a bone, she would not stop crying and we would know it." This is so true, except the internet is filled with stories of freak accidents and stories about kids who sneeze and then three days later their eyes explode and if that mom had only known and read that Facebook post warning about sneezes, then her child would not be blinded by that sneeze! The horror!!! I know this sounds far-fetched to those of you without anxiety or those of you who are not in mommy groups seeing these posts about all of the things that ARE GOING TO HURT YOUR CHILDREN UNLESS YOU READ THIS! It is really hard to not worry, but all of the times Molly got hurt, we would be able to get her to calm down quickly, and the next day I would usually forget about it and all would be right with the world again.

In January of 2019, Philip left the job he had at our church and started working with his dad in the construction business. It was a move we had prayed about and thought about for a long time. We were both excited about it, but it was a big change for us. He came home for lunch every day while he was at the church, and it was a closer commute and a later start to his day. The change took some getting used to but we did. Our kids adjusted accordingly by waking up in the 6 AM hour to see him off. Winter of 2019 went by slowly. It was cold, it was snowy, and my baby did not nap. We stayed home a lot, and I looked forward to spring. Spring meant getting outside and going for walks. Fresh air and sunshine would surely lift my spirits.

One day in March it was nice and sunny, so someone close to the family asked if they could take Molly to the park. I agreed since Ander still was not doing well in the nap department and it would be nice to have a break once I finally got him to go down. I had just got Ander down for a nap when my phone rang; it was Philip. I answered, and he said, "Hey, I don't want you to freak out but.." Instantly my heart dropped and my stomach felt sick. "Molly and our close friend were going down the slide and her foot got caught, and now she won't stop crying so they are on their way back home to see if you can calm her down." He did not even finish his sentence before my head was whirling. I was going through my mental checklist of things that meant this was not going to be good. A phone call, not a text. Check. She will not stop crying - this is how we know something is really wrong. Check. She was going down the slide on the lap of an adult - and one of those warnings from Facebook popped into my head. "NEVER GO DOWN THE SLIDE WITH YOUR CHILD ON YOUR LAP," it read. "THEY WILL BREAK THEIR LEG," it warned. Of course, I'd thought that was a freak accident and never thought about warning my child's caregivers about it. CHECK, CHECK, CHECK. I knew it, she had a broken leg. Philip was more level-headed and figured if I could get her to settle down, then she was fine. I hung up the phone and started to get dressed to take my daughter to the doctor. My phone rang again. It was the close friend. "Mary...every bump makes her cry; I think we need to take her to the ER." My stomach sank again, and I started thinking about deductibles and what if I was overreacting and she did not actually break her leg; a trip to the ER would be so expensive. When they got home, I ran out to the car and talked to Molly. She was crying and did not want anyone near her leg. I told her we needed to go to a doctor. She started sobbing harder and saying she did NOT want a doctor to touch her leg. I reached for her buckle, and she cried harder still. I knew this was something different than anything we'd seen before.

I jumped in the car and drove to the ER. All the while thinking about them having to perform surgery on my daughter or setting her leg, but also thinking maybe I was overreacting. I got to the ER and sat in the parking lot and called my friend Oralia. I told her what was going on and asked her to pray with me and for me. She did and then suggested I go to an urgent care with an X-ray machine. It would be cheaper, and if it was not broken we would avoid a trip to the ER. I thought that sounded like a good idea, so we went to the closest urgent care with an X-ray machine. I carried her in and began filling out the paperwork. They called me up to the desk and told me they did not take my insurance and it would be very expensive if we stayed there. I picked up Molly and started taking her back to the car. She started sobbing and saying she just wanted to see a doctor to help her feel better.

We found another urgent care that took our insurance and had an X-ray machine. I picked up Philip, who thankfully had left work and came with us. We got to the waiting room, and Molly was totally calm. She was excited that we were letting her play a game on my phone and was not crying at all. We started to think maybe it was just a sprain or she had overreacted. So we asked her if she wanted to walk over to the drinking fountain, but she refused to put any weight on her leg, not even her toe. We looked at each other, and we both knew she was hurt. When we got back to the room, the doctor looked at her leg and pushed on it and she did not even flinch. When she bent her leg, she flinched a little but kept playing the game on my phone. We all thought maybe she sprained her knee since it got twisted on the slide, but the doctor wanted to take X-rays just to be safe. Philip stayed with her in the X-ray room, and I sat in the hall and filled in friends and family on what had been going on. She was a little nervous, but Philip did an amazing job at keeping her occupied, and she was really brave.

We went back to our room and waited for the doctor to get the results. I started to feel better, like it was just an accident at the park and with some rest and maybe some ice, she would be good to go. When the doctor came back in, I knew by the look on her face that was not the case. She had broken her tibia. My stomach, which had returned to its normal place, once again sank into my feet. It was a clean break, and she would not need surgery. Which was a huge relief. She set her in a splint and told us in 3 days we would go to an orthopedic doctor to get a hard cast. They put them in splints because swelling can cause them to lose circulation, which can lead to things like loss of limb. No big deal. Ha.

We took her home and she sat on the couch for the rest of the day. She was hurting and tired from all of the excitement. We rotated her meds, and she did alright. Going to the bathroom the first day was really hard because her leg was so sensitive and not able to bend, so we had to figure some things out. We woke her up to give her pain meds, but she was so tired she barely noticed. By the next evening, she was feeling well enough to go to AWANA. Philip put her in an umbrella stroller and pushed her around the whole night. Her friends had brought her gifts and cards and prayed with her in class. She really loved seeing her friends.

That night she woke up crying so we gave her pain meds. Then every 20 minutes for the rest of the night she would cry out in pain. I laid in her bed with her and tried to comfort her, but she could not be settled. I started panicking, thinking circulation was being cut off. She came into our bed with us, which she hardly ever gets to do and usually solves any and all problems, but it did not work. I just held her and cried and prayed that her pain would go away all night. She was crying, I was crying, but I had to remain calm for her.

In the morning when Philip had to go to work, I told him I could not be left alone with her because she needed constant attention and Ander needed me too. He called his mom and she came out very early in the morning so I could have help with the kids. Even with Mimi there, watching a movie, and eating whatever she wanted, she could not be comforted. She wanted me to hold her, so I picked her up and rocked her while she sobbed. I asked her where it hurt, and she pointed to her ankle. Her ankle? Maybe they missed something and her ankle needed to be set! I called the nurse hotline from our insurance company, and they suggested based on what I had told them that she should go to the ER. "What if I went back to the urgent care?" "You already tried that and they've done all they can do for you there. You need to go to the ER."

So after Ander woke up, I fed him and left him with Mimi to look after him, and we went to the ER. Something I never wanted to do as a parent, but something a lot of parents do, and in a lot worse situations. I know I should be grateful, but nothing prepares you for that moment when you wheel your crying toddler into a hospital Emergency Room. After a lot of doctors came in and out and asked us a lot of questions, they took off her splint and looked at her leg. As soon as her splint was off, she was happy and didn't talk about her leg. My sister and nephew were already coming to visit us; when I called her en route to the ER, they came and brought us breakfast and coffee. Russell helped entertain Molly while we waited, and Laura helped keep me occupied and calm while we waited. I am so grateful that they were already planning on coming and that Laura is so selfless and came to the ER to visit us. When I took Molly back for X-rays, the super sweet X-ray tech realized that she had a huge sore on her heel and told me to make sure the doctor saw it.

Eventually, it was just Molly and I again in the room. It was determined that her pain was caused from not enough padding in her splint and her heel had rubbed against the splint so much it caused a pressure ulcer. Imagine having a really bad blister on your heel, but never being able to take your shoe off and not understanding what a blister is and why you are in so much pain. This was why she was hysterical for hours. The ER doc told me Molly had to stop eating her donuts because she was going to need to be sedated to put her cast on her. Sedated?? The thought of that was just heartbreaking! When the orthopedic doctor came in, he let his resident put Molly's cast on. I asked at what point she would need to be sedated. He looked at me like I was crazy and told me they did not need to sedate her because she was calm and doing great. I love it when doctors do not communicate and tell you the worst-case scenario. I mean, why even bother throwing in a "might" or "there is a chance"? It is probably best to just make statements even when you do not know anything for sure. This really helps parents feel relaxed and calm.

The resident put Molly's cast on, but it was definitely her first rodeo and she had to take it off and start again. The yanking motion of the wet cast coming off hurt Molly, so I was just thrilled when the doctor told her she could try again. At the end of the day, Molly had a bright pink cast and was ready to go home. He told us she was not allowed to walk on it at all and she could maybe get it off in 2 weeks. We got a referral to a different orthopedic practice than we originally had because the hospital we went to was a different network of hospitals. I had called Molly's primary care doctor to get a referral for the first orthopedic practice, and when I called again for a second referral, they were not having it. They told me they had let it go the first time even though she had not come in, but they would not do that again. So, since I obviously was making this whole thing up, I had to go in to their office for them to see that her leg was, in fact, broken before they would give us a referral for a follow-up visit. Their office is an hour away from our house, which I suppose is not their fault; the average person probably sees a local pediatrician or primary doctor - not us. We are too extra for that. Just kidding; I just do not like any of the doctors I have seen around us and this place was recommended to me. Since we do not go to the doctor very often, I figured it would not be a big deal. I was super annoyed in that moment, but when we went, they let us do her 3-year well visit instead of coming back in a month to do it. So, all in all, it was not that bad.

Once we finally got the referral to the orthopedic doctor, she got an X-ray. They told us that if she felt like it, she could walk on it, and we needed to come back in 4 weeks for her cast to be off. Over the next 4 weeks, she crawled, scooted, climbed, cruised, walked, and even jumped in her cast. The bottom of it was crushed and muddy by the time we went in for our follow-up visit. By this time, Molly was a pro and knew how these visits go. "We go get a Ex-Ka-Ray, then go back to the room and wait," basically. Except for this time they turned on a very loud saw to cut off her cast. We tried to prepare her, but when they started moving it toward her, she lost her mind. Understandably so. After the cast was off, she got her "EX KA RAY." The doctor told us that her leg was 90% healed but not enough damage to justify putting a cast back on, so we left with it off and had to come back in a month.

She walked with a limp for almost an entire month. She dragged her foot around like a dead fish behind her. When we got home from taking her cast off, I put her in jeans for the first time in a month and I cried a little. I never realized how much I missed that little jeaned bum running around my house. Each day her leg got better and better, and we put it behind us. Now she runs and jumps like nothing ever happened. Though it is something we have not forgotten. Whenever we drive by the park where she broke her

133

leg, which is at least once a week, she will point out the window and say, "That is the park where I broke my leg." Daily we play "doctor;" Philip, myself, or one of Molly's baby dolls will break their leg and we will have to call the doctor. The doctor will have us come to his/her office and we will have to hold the patient's hand while we listen to their heart, then go get an EX KA RAY. It is always a broken bone, never a sprain. Then we put a cast on or a bandage, the patient goes home and returns a few weeks (read minutes) later, and we take the cast off. Then another one of her babies will get hurt and we will have to do the same game over again. I sometimes ask her if she has guard rails or if anyone is even watching her babies at home; she always tells me no. I tell her I may have to call CPS on her; I am so judgmental.

So, yeah. I guess you could say the worst case scenario that I dreamed up in my head did come true. But here is what I learned from all of that - it changed nothing. Even though I was afraid of Molly getting hurt, that did not stop it from happening. It really did not help the situation, even though in my anxious mind I thought maybe it would. It just made me unhappier before it happened. And ya know what else? She is okay. Yes, she broke her leg, but it could have been worse. If it was more serious, we would have gotten through it. Kids are more resilient than you think. I mean, if you see a mom, midwife or doctor pull a baby out, you know they are not as delicate as they seem. Molly is no worse off because it happened to her, and I did nothing to prevent it from happening. Does that mean I don't worry about my kids? No way. Does that mean I don't have worst case scenarios jump in my head all the time? Nope, I still do. Does that mean my anxiety is gone? Nope. But is it better? You betcha. Even though I still have anxiety about a lot of things - some rational, some not so rational - I actually am able to talk myself down a lot quicker now. My kids jump on the couch sometimes, they jump on the bed, but I don't envision them getting concussions anymore. I know it could happen, and I know they could break their limbs. But I also know every day kids are jumping on furniture and getting out unscathed. So I have let go of my need to be in control a little. It gets better every day. Unless you put me on an airplane - then I will spend the entire flight counting down the minutes until we land and telling myself, "Airplanes don't just blow up. Airplanes don't just blow up," every few minutes throughout the flight. Anxiety is a giant in my life that I hope to one day completely slay; but for now, I remember Molly's broken leg and take one more baby step toward that goal.

Chapter 18

BODY AFTER BABY

After I had Molly, I got into pretty good shape from working out. Though my belly button would never recover. With Ander, however, my pregnancy went an entire week longer, and I worked out through my entire pregnancy and, well, my belly button and stomach were never going to recover from that. I lost almost all of my baby weight pretty fast, but I started to realize I still had a "cone" under my stomach. I performed a test on myself to see if I had Diastasis Recti, and I did; by my calculations I had a 3-finger separation. Diastasis Recti, or "DR" as I will henceforth call it, is a separation of the abdominal walls. It can happen with rapid weight gain, c-sections, and in a lot of pregnancies. I knew I had it a little bit after Ander was born, but I thought I could figure it out on my own. I was supposed to wear a brace while exercising, but it was so hot that most of the time I did not wear it. I found a program online, but it told me to stop all other exercise while healing and doing the therapy program, so I did not want to do that. I wanted to finish the Open (a worldwide online CrossFit competition) with all of my friends at my gym before I was going to stop. I tried to do the online program, but for the life of me, I could not fire the muscles it was talking about. I decided to take the plunge and go to physical therapy. I had to go to my OB-GYN and my primary doctor (you know, the one an hour from my house) to get a referral for a pelvic floor specialist, but no one had any idea of where to find one! I searched the internet high and low, and I could not find one. I finally just Googled "physical therapy near me" and found the closest office and called to see if maybe they could refer me somewhere. Turns out they had a Pelvic Floor PT on staff. I started going to her in March and as of July, I was still going to her. I thought I would take four weeks off and be back at it. It turns out I had really ripped my abs open. My separation was about 5.5 inches long and 2.5 to 3 fingers wide. I closed my gap to 1.5 to 2.5 from top to bottom. I had to wear a brace 12 hours a day and do exercises 3 times a day. It was annoying, but I lost inches off my waist in just a few weeks. After that my progress slowed; I still am seeing some progress but not as much. I slowly got clearance to add more and more weight, but I can only lift 12-pound weights and I still cannot do any high impact.

I ended up quitting our CrossFit gym. Not only were we paying a lot of money every month, I was barely doing anything close to CrossFit, and with Philip's new work schedule we were not able to make it more than one or two times a week if we were lucky. We decided to stop. I was so down about my body that I wanted to give up working out anyway. I know that you may look at me and think I am crazy for hating my body, but I do. I wish I could write this from a standpoint of loving my body and being proud of it. Well, to a certain degree I can say that. I have stretch marks all over my stomach, and I am really proud of those. I carried two babies in me, and I was pregnant longer than anyone I know. But my stomach is far from flat, and I absolutely hate looking at myself from the side. Truthfully, I feel hopeless about it. I have been in physical therapy for months, and I have stalled out on my progress. I have poured hundreds of dollars into my therapy, and I feel like it will never get better. I see my DR cone in every picture of myself; every time I look in the mirror it glares at me.

On top of that, I have so much extra skin from having the giant bellies that it just hangs there. There are times I look in the mirror and I just look at myself in disgust. I say all of this because this is what goes on in my head; if I am having these thoughts then maybe there is someone out there who is going through that too. Instead of sitting here and telling you to be proud of your body and give yourself grace, I think I want to tell you that it is okay to notice those changes. Because your body is different after having babies. Some people bounce right back, and I have a lot of friends who look amazing after babies. But when I ask them about their bodies or mention mine, they say, "Yeah, mine looks bad too." YOURS?? You wear a bikini! Your abs meet in the middle! You are tiny! You don't look like you're pregnant still! You have no extra skin! But they have imperfections, and they see them every time they look in the mirror or at a picture of themselves. Maybe now I will have 10 Beachbody coaches reach out to me and want to help me. I kid, I kid. I actually think Beachbody is great, but I can't do very many of the programs so it frustrates me. Maybe I should eat clean or count calories or my macros. Maybe I should just embrace my body for where I am. Give myself grace for bringing two of the cutest humans into the world. But I am not in either of those places. I am in the place of working really hard on being a mom, while fighting depression and anxiety, trying to spend one on one time with my kids, date my incredible husband, and write a book. I feel like I have so many things on my heart that having a six-pack is just not one of them. I actually worked really hard on having a healthy relationship with food. I have always been good at listening to my body and knowing when to stop. I know how I feel when I eat my vegetables and cleaner foods. But I also know what burgers taste like. I know that when it is summertime, I want to get ice cream all the time.

I think it's about balance and moderation, and I have come a long way from where I was. I don't even mean with my diet, though I never ate vegetables until I was 20 years old. Not even one. I think I would be a lot taller if I had eaten my fruits and veggies growing up. I don't even mean with loving my body; I think I have come a long way knowing that this is where I am. I want a tummy tuck one day, and I am not ashamed about that. Is it a waste of money and vain? Maybe. But it is something I want. It would fix my DR forever and get rid of all of the wrinkles on my stomach. If I ever got one, I would tell you about it. I would not lie to you. This still is not where I start to go into a motivational speech about our bodies and being a mom and a woman. I am not there, and I am here to tell you that if you are not there either, then I am right there with you. So we can stand next to each other and find our best angle in pictures and find an exercise program that we enjoy and then eat some vegetables that taste good to us. We can do that, or we can get overwhelmed with being moms and go get ice cream and want a tummy tuck. Or a boob lift. These are not bad things - these are our lives and our thoughts.

Chapter 19

POSTPARTUM

This is the part of the book I never thought I would write. When I started writing this book, this was never a thought in my mind. Now, this is the part of the book I am most scared to write. If you believe in God or spiritual warfare, you may understand that the closer I came to writing this part of the book, the harder I struggled with this. Maybe by telling my story and sharing my journey, someone out there will read it and not feel alone, or go get help. I don't know. Maybe it was all a coincidence, and I just am struggling and writing is really emotionally hard to do. Especially when you are still going through it. I am still going through it, though I believe I am on the downslope of it. I still have bad days, and I still wish I could be better and that my husband did not have to worry about me. But I am not there yet; I am on the road there. The road I am talking about is postpartum depression. I often say to myself I am postpartum depressed. As I have said before, I am a doula and I know what the risk factors for postpartum depression are. There is a huge hormonal side of things, but there are outside factors that can contribute and lead to Postpartum Depression (PPD). If you know me in real life, you may have no idea that I have dealt and still am honestly dealing with what I am about to share here. Probably because I do not want to be dealing with what I am going to share about. I wish I could pretend it was not happening, that I was stronger than this, that it did not happen to me. Because it makes me feel like I am crazy and weak. I will back up and start at the beginning, a very good place to start.

Postpartum

When I had Molly, I had postpartum anxiety (PPA), but I was able to deal with that on my own. When I was pregnant with Ander, I knew that PPD and/or PPA could happen to me. I thought I was prepared. Once he was born, I accepted help, and I let things go around the house, and I was okay with it; I was prepared for it. I was exhausted and cranky, but I just brushed it all off, chalked it up to just "being tired." After all, having a newborn is hard. As Ander got older and sleep had its ups and downs, I was not really finding a lot of relief. I was overwhelmed by my kids and my house. All aspects of life were starting to get more and more daunting. I wanted to have it all together. We had decided we were done having kids, because the newborn phase was just impossible for us. Which, again, was sooner than I ever expected, and that failure hung over my head like a dark cloud. I felt like my time was split too much between my two kids, and Molly was watching way more TV than I ever wanted her to. Every day I tried to be better; every day I tried to pay attention to each kid, but every day the weight of it all sunk down heavier on me. I tried to fix it all on my own, even though Philip was right there and willing and ready to help me with whatever I needed. I did not want to admit that I needed help, because I'd always wanted to be a mom; and now I was a mom, and I only had two kids. Some people have 4 kids, 5 kids, 6 kids, and they have it all down. I should be able to do all of this. I just needed to try harder and figure out the sleep thing, and then I would be fine. In my mind, sleep was the key to every part of my life falling back into place.

I searched the internet for hours to help with Ander's sleep, and everything told me I needed him to get on a schedule and he should not be nursing to sleep. I had literally spent hours crying and praying that he would fall asleep, and when he finally fell asleep nursing - and not being bounced all night - I felt like freedom was coming. Now everything was telling me that nursing was why he did not nap, because he couldn't nurse to sleep then. Nursing to sleep is "wrong." So I had no choice but to keep searching. I found some gentle methods to ease him out of nursing to sleep. But with that came a schedule. I would try a schedule, and he still would only take 30 minute

144

naps, which according to sleep experts does not even count as a nap. So now what do I do? I just had to try harder. I ordered and read books, read blogs, tried different apps on my phone - all of it. He was not sleeping, and I felt stuck at home for days at a time. When I would throw caution to the wind and try to have him sleep in the car or in a stroller (like so many people can do), he would barely sleep. That night he would be up for hours. My anxious thoughts and fears came true. I was right. I had to stay at home.

Not only that, but Molly had to be quiet anytime Ander was asleep. We have a tiny house, so I ended up letting her watch TV during his naps. Which added to the mounting guilt. I follow so many moms on Instagram who do not even have a TV. "Okay," I would tell myself, "this is just a season; we just need to make it through this season." But this season did not seem to be ending, and I got more and more overwhelmed. Soon I was canceling plans because I was just too overwhelmed to leave the house. I was sinking further down into a depression, and I did not even realize it. I had the shortest fuse, and I flat out did not enjoy being a mom. I was terrible at it, and I hated it. I said this in my head and, as much as it pains me to admit, I said it out loud to my baby, "I hate this. I hate this. Why won't you sleep? Why can't I do this? I hate this. I hate it. I think I might hate you." Then I would instantly hate myself for saying that. But I could not stop it. I was in this cycle I did not know how to and could not break out of. I just wanted him to sleep so I could enjoy my kids and do something as simple as play outside, and I couldn't even do that. I didn't have any way to relieve stress at the time. Bible Study was on break, and I wasn't working out because of this stupid injury that made me hate the way I looked. I was isolated. I was isolating myself, but I did not see it that way at the time.

A few times Ander would take a 20 minute nap, and I saw my entire day being over and knew I would be up for hours that night. The exhaustion was hitting me preemptively. I would literally change into pajamas and be done. This "season," as they say, was just not going to end, and I hated it. And I hated myself.

Postpartum

There were times Philip would come home and I would get in bed until it was time to put Ander to sleep; I would get up, put him down, and get back in bed. Maybe I needed a break from my kids, maybe I was tired, but this - this was not healthy. One time we were supposed to go somewhere as a family, but I just did not want to. I could not explain why, I just could not muster the energy to do it. Not even enough energy to put on a brave face and fake it, and so I just laid on the couch. Molly cried and wanted me to come with them. My precious, caring toddler did not understand. I dug down deep and went with them. I had fun, but then I had all of this guilt that I had put my daughter through that. There would be times when I could not get off the couch. I wanted to take my kids to the park, but I needed to get dressed. But by the time I got everyone dressed and fed and looking good, it would be time to put someone down for a nap. So why even bother? I would just stay in my pajamas. We stayed inside all of the time.

One time Philip tried to get me to come to the park with them, but I was so overwhelmed I did not want to. I think, honestly, I just did not want to be with my kids. My husband would come home from a long, hard day at work and put the kids in the car and be an amazing parent. It made me hate myself, because I couldn't do that. I was failing. I laid in my bed while they were at the park and cried. I started to think thoughts that really scared me. Not about killing myself - I never wanted to do that. But I really thought my family would be better off if I was gone. I could not stop yelling at them; that's trauma. I laid in bed and did not want to go anywhere; that's trauma. Molly watched TV for hours; that's terrible. I would think I hated my children. I would say, alone to myself or out loud to Philip, "I hate being a mom."

These things I am describing are not okay things to think, do, or say, and I was doing them. So I thought leaving them would be better than putting them through this over and over. And I made a plan to do it. My plan was that I would send a text to our pastor and his wife and tell them, "I am leaving Philip; he is going to need support," then leave my phone on the counter so he could not track me, with a note saying, "I hope he takes formula for you," and then go to the ATM and take some money out.

I had a plan. This is what PPD does to you. It lies to you. It won't let you think about what your kids will say when your husband tries to explain why Mom left. It doesn't let you think about your son who will not take a bottle. It blinds you to the pain you will put your husband through. All you can think about is if I can't get him to sleep or her to listen to me, then I might as well just leave and maybe someone can do it better than me.

I had those thoughts, but I couldn't make a plan on where I would go after I got the money. And honestly, there are not a lot of places I could get without GPS on my phone. I closed my eyes and prayed, "God, I need help." That was it; that was all I prayed. I still laid in bed and tried to come up with the next part of my plan. But as hard as I tried, I couldn't think of what would be a good next step. I wanted God to direct me to a person that I could drive to. All of a sudden, I got a bolt of energy, and I jumped out of bed and tried to go out and see my family playing outside. I was excited that I was beating Depression. But Depression was louder than my thoughts, and after just a few steps it told me to turn around, and I did. And two times I got back in bed, then back out. If God was going to help me, it was going to be another day; today I was going to be in bed. The next day it happened again. But I was lying on my couch while my children played together. I just kept trying to come up with where to go. Who would take me in? I prayed again "Lord, I need help," and in that moment, He broke through the depression. I jumped up and said to myself, "This is not okay! I am not okay." When Philip came home, I started sobbing to him. Depression was still yelling in my ear, "He doesn't care! He is not going to help you! He should leave your sorry self!" So what came out was a mix of lies and truth. I looked at Philip and said, "I am not okay! And I do not understand why you don't care that I am not okay!"

He looked at me stunned and said, "Of course I care! Let's figure this out!"
"I just need him to sleep!"
"Okay, we can hire a sleep consultant, and you need to go see Jill."

So we made a plan. I was going to hire a sleep consultant and go see my midwife. I wish I could say it was done and I was better the next day. It was not. I did hire a sleep consultant, but it would be a few days before I talked to them. I felt slightly better knowing relief was on the way. I thought I was cured. Okay, cool, mildly depressed - that's not too bad. I was not too crazy. Even still, I almost canceled the call multiple times. I think because it was sort of a last resort, and I did not want to try my last resort and have it not work. Then I surely would run away.

My doula from Ander's birth "happened" to post some signs of depression and mental illness on her doula Facebook page. "Canceling plans. Mood Swings." Oh my gosh, that is me! Maybe I am not just a horrible person; maybe this is something in me, happening to me. Okay, I would keep the sleep consultant call. But the reminders of my failure were everywhere. My 3-year-old would say, "Mom, where were you when my dad took me to a park? Oh, you were in bed." I never wanted her to say that again. I was motivated to get better, and the truth was starting to break through the lies of Depression. But Depression was loud and heavy. And I felt ashamed that it was even there. I tried to ignore it. I would make a plan to get better, and then I would think it would not work, so I would just give up. At least I was not failing; I was just quitting. I could live with that.

Philip urged me to text Jill and go in and see her. It took multiple times of typing out, "I think I am struggling with Postpartum Depression and I need help" before I ever sent it. Admitting it was admitting weakness. When I finally did it, I sobbed. She replied that she would absolutely help me, but I needed to contact her assistant to make an appointment. That took me another few hours to do. Once I finally got an appointment time, I canceled it. I did not want to get a babysitter and tell them where I was going. If people knew that I had PPD, they would think I was crazy and they would baby or pity me. I would not allow that. So I actually never even went to the appointment. I still have not gone to see her. When I have bad days, Philip tells me I need to call her. I tell him I know what she will say - take time for myself, work out; I can do that on my own.

I did not know who to tell; I didn't want to tell anyone, but I knew I had to tell people. I told Laura. And she was wonderful about it. She listened, did not judge, did not make me feel crazy. She told me about a supplement to take. She asked if I thought I should get on antidepressants. She assured me that it did not have to be forever and I could find one I liked. I told her I did not want to go there yet, but I knew I would if I had to. When I am having a bad day I tell her about it, and she is incredible about making me feel like I am not crazy and I am not alone in this. I told my mom, and she was understanding and listened. My mom has 3 kids, and she did it all without help. But she told me it's okay to get help and it's okay to take medicine if I need it. Even though she had raised her 3 kids without much help - my dad worked long hours - and she did a great job with us, she still told me asking for help was okay. I thought she would think less of me.

After I had my appointment with the sleep consultant, Ander's sleep got better. I had 4 days of not feeling depressed. My outlook on life shifted, and I felt better. Truthfully, I thought it was over. But then a few days later, Ander had a really bad nap and I slipped. I slipped hard. I tried to fight it, but I ended up in bed again. I didn't know what to say to Philip. But I closed my eyes and prayed that God would help me. I hadn't eaten dinner yet, and try as I might, I was not able to sleep until I ate. I went out into the kitchen and got some food and asked Philip to sit with me. I started crying and said, "I thought I was better." He said he knew it was not over. I had better days because Ander was sleeping. I needed to have a bad day and not fall into depression; then he would know I was better. I asked if he was worried about me. He said of course he was. I said I never think or want to kill myself. He said he would still have to keep an eye on me. I cried again. "I don't want your life to have to be like this. You do not deserve this. I would understand if you left me."

He told me he would never leave me. He knew I struggled with Anxiety and Depression when he married me. I cried again. I love him. I love that man so much. He is my best friend in the whole world, and I put him through so much. But he never falters. He never yells back when I am yelling. He pushes me to get help and assures me it is okay. I need to get better for my kids, yes, without a doubt. But I WANT to be better for Philip. I want to be carefree and go on dates and go on trips. I don't want to have these mood swings and switch what I want or need every 5 minutes. But I do. I am on a journey to get better, and he is walking right beside me.

I keep making plans for my road to recovery, but I have not fully followed through with any of them because they are so overwhelming. I keep thinking I am better, but then I slip. But each time I slip less and less down into Depression's grip. I had a really bad day not too long ago, but I did not end up in bed. I did want to go to work full-time so I did not have to see my kids. My next thought was that I could not possibly want to go to work because I was supposed to want to be around my kids. I had dreamed of being a mom my entire life, and now I felt like I was not doing a good job. Plus Mr. Anxiety was telling me that no one else could watch my kids without them getting hurt or ruining Ander's nap schedule. I did not enjoy being a mom; I hated not enjoying it. Depression told me that I have never liked being a mom, ever. That this hard day was all day, every day, and I wasn't a good mom. Depression was drowning out all of the good times and the good moments. Making it impossible to see through the bad to the good.

I texted Philip and told him about my terrible day. Philip told me I was a good mom but it was hard being a mom. So I listed all of the reasons why, on the contrary, I am a really bad mom. He replied back, "Ok, but you're their Mom; do you believe God made a mistake?"

Postpartum

Truthfully, other than praying for help in those darkest moments, I had not thought much about my faith in all of this. Though I am a Christian and I want Christ to be in every part of my life, I had not thought about how He factored into all of this. I thought if I just read my Bible (heck, I even taught a study), worshipped God, and went to church, then I did not need Him in this part of me. I never thought about how prideful I was being. How I was trying to do this on my own. I admit that I did not want His help, because I felt like I should be able to do this alone. Of course, God got the credit when everything was going well because He was helping me through it. But what about every single moment in between? When Ander did not nap or when Molly talked back? Was He there then? Did I need Him then? Didn't I used to teach in my study about relying on God every second of every day? Why is this, this Depression, this part of me any different? Why am I keeping this from Him? I am getting better at relying on Him and giving this to Him every second of the day when I am struggling. If I believe He does not make mistakes, then I have to believe He gave me these kids on purpose and He is helping me. Friend, stop trying to dig your heels in deeper. Stop thinking you just need to try harder and it will all get better. Please, I urge you, take a step back!

Philip told me to have his mom come and help me with the kids. I did not want to, but I knew I needed to so I accepted the help. A few minutes later I changed my mind. I wanted to sleep in, and I did not want help from anyone anymore. I was fine. I could do it. He told me I absolutely needed this and if I did not accept the help that he would drive me to Jill's office and make me get help. After praying and thinking about it and talking to Laura, I decided to let her come and help me one day. Philip thanked me and asked me to trust his lead in this family.

The morning that she came I was excited about the help. But inside I could feel Depression kicking and screaming. "You do not need help. You should want to be with your kids 24/7. Why did you become a mom if you were just going to fail at it? You only have two kids and you can't do this? You are so weak." I looked in the mirror as I got ready, and I thought to myself, 'No, you are not weak. You are going to get so much stuff done when she is here." I let her come, and I got out of the house and saw a friend. I did not let Depression win that time, though she was kicking and screaming.

Every day is a battle, and I long for the day when I do not have to think, "I am having a really good day." I just want it to be my norm. That is just not where I am. If you are having any signs or symptoms of PPD or PPA, please reach out to someone. Reach out to a mom friend, your mom, a not-mom friend, your spouse, even to me, anyone. No one will think you are crazy. They will feel honored that you let them into your journey. They will be glad you let them into your thoughts. What you bring into the light can't be hidden. Those thoughts you are having are probably not true and when you voice them, write them down, type them out, it is easier to process them. The more you keep it in, the louder the thoughts become and the harder it is to combat them with the truth. Get help. Go to your doctor or midwife, it is okay to be on medication for some amount of time. This does not mean you are weak or a bad mom. It does not matter if you have 1 kid or 6 kids. Being a mom is hard, and there is constant pressure from all sides to have it all together and to enjoy every second of being a mom. You are honestly just not going to.

And there are going to be well-meaning older moms who tell you to "find the joy." "Enjoy it now; it goes by quick," or, "You're going to miss this." It's like - listen, Linda, we get it. We know. Your kids are older and you miss them being little, but don't pretend like you loved every second of this. And do not pressure me to enjoy this. Because when your kid is pooping and your baby is trying to throw a toothbrush in the toilet and then they both start screaming when you remove them from the situation, that is not a fun moment. It just is not. So don't sugar coat it and make me feel bad that I did not think about how funny that is. Here's an idea: don't say anything. Or if you feel compelled to say something, offer some words like, "It's hard, I know." "You're doing a good job," or even, "You may laugh at this later, but right now it is really hard."

Like Philip told me - you are their mom. And if you believe in God, then you have to know that you did not get here by accident. And if you do not believe in God - then whatever your worldview is - know that this is the way that it is and your kids look up to you no matter what. They need YOU. YOU MATTER TO THEM. They don't care if you are tired, no makeup, don't go outside much, they watch TV more than someone else; they think you are the bee's knees, and do not let Depression tell you any differently.

Chapter 20

WHY I DECIDED TO WRITE THIS BOOK

I think one of the biggest reasons why I wrote this book is because, simply, I have always wanted to. I used to love going to the library or bookstore with my mom and sister and getting books. I read all the time, and I started trying to write books at a very young age. I remember I had a folder of characters that I was going to use in my book series. I was nothing short of ambitious. But life happens, you doubt yourself, you get busy and move on. The thought and dream have always been in my head. I even paid $1,000 to take an online book writing class. I ended up utilizing their money-back guarantee, because I could not come up with an idea. They said "from no idea to best-selling book." I didn't even have an idea, so I cancelled it. I remember the minute I decided to write a book. I was at a bowling alley with my church, and a sweet friend said, "I love your Facebook posts - you should write a book!" That was it. Apparently, all I needed was one outside source telling me to go for it. And I did.

Looking back to my first attempts at writing books, I think the problem was that I did not know my passion yet. I am now a mom of two and love everything mom-related. I love pregnancy, labor, birth, babies, and raising kids. I have found that this is my passion. For me personally, having a baby in the house is beyond hard and something I don't plan on doing again, but I love talking about it. I love starting, changing, and having conversations about motherhood. Motherhood is isolating. It can be, anyway. I think as my story in motherhood started to unravel, I started writing this book in my head. I doubt my ability to write almost every day. I go back and forth between wanting to do this and thinking it is a waste. Thinking that I will just be embarrassed because not a soul will read it. But I also really want to do this. I think people might think I am dumb for thinking that my story was worth telling. But I know that isn't true, because I firmly believe every person has a story worth telling.

I have dabbled in blogging countless times. I love writing and blogging. But to be a successful blogger, you need to have consistent and catchy content. That got to be forced after a while; I was always trying to figure out how to be a better blogger and reach more people. I didn't want to think in blog posts. I did not want to think about my social media accounts, I wanted to spend time with my kids and live my life. In writing this book and telling my story all at once rather than continually and in shorter bursts, I was able to do it on my time. It took me several months to write this book. I would write every day for a few days, then not write again for weeks. Some of this story unfolded as I was writing it. Molly had not even broken her leg the first time I started writing this. It feels more organic this way, this is my life in real-time. This is not a sponsored post, an ad, or a post I needed to get out so I did not lose my audience. This is on my time, in my voice, when I wanted.

I don't want this to be a self-help book. This isn't a motivational book per se. I don't have a lot of advice to give you about being a good mom, because I never know if I am doing this right. Kids, at least mine, did not come with instruction manuals. I think for a lot of things with kids, there is no black and white. There are a lot of gray areas. Yes, of course, there are some things that are straight-up yes and no. But truth be told, many things can vary from person to person based on what they hold dear and their belief system. I think I often find myself wondering if I am doing this mom thing right, or if there is a better way of doing it. I think that is what makes me a good mom. Even when I feel like I am screwing them both up, I know deep down I am a good mom. I think if you're trying - you are a good mom. I think. I mean, you can probably come up with exceptions to that rule. But why ya gotta go and ruin this for me? I am trying to be encouraging.

I wanted to be honest and tell my story with all the good and all the bad. We are all different, we don't all raise our kids the same, we don't follow nap times and schedules, we let daycare workers and church volunteers watch our kids, we can't dream of letting another soul watch our babies, we vaccinate, we don't vaccinate, we stay home, we go to work, we have c-sections, we have vaginal births, we breastfeed, we bottle feed. The list goes on and on. We all do it differently, and maybe there is a jerk out there who judges you for your choices. But my friend, my friend, they are not going to tell that to your face. They really are not. They may tell you on the internet, so maybe we shouldn't be on the internet. Maybe they are going to say it behind your back, but then maybe their opinion doesn't matter. Or maybe, JUST maybe, they actually do not think about you as much as you think they do. Their world probably does not revolve around you as much as you are afraid it does.

Speaking of the internet - I recently put a poll on my Instagram asking other moms to fill me in on whether or not they have ever used outside help with watching their kids. If they had or hadn't, and if they wished their answer was different. At first, the majority of the responses were that everyone used help or wanted to use help, and I was super encouraged. As more and more results came in, more people started to say, "Nah, I am good." Truthfully, it was crushing to see some moms say they are good. I was afraid of that happening. It solidified in my mind that I was the weaker mom. I took a step back and looked closer at the results. A lot of moms I look up to and admire said they asked for help when their kids were younger. I had no idea. From looking at their social media pages, I would never have guessed they got help. But maybe that's just it - they were using help and that is what made them seem like they were doing it with grace and ease.

It also occurred to me that it is okay that some moms do not want help. Maybe those are the moms that can do the helping. Maybe some seasons of life are just easier for others. We are all different, no one parents the exact same way, and that is okay. I think another thing that stops us from getting help is that if we admit we need help, that allows someone to peek into our messy houses, messy lives and see our reality, and we get immediately defensive of the way we are doing things. We think, "They're going to judge me because XYZ." Maybe it's that you don't shower everyday. Or your kids eat candy for breakfast. Maybe, like me, there are days you don't like your kids. Yes, you love them and would maul a rabid raccoon if it came near your baby. But sometimes they is whiny. And if someone is there helping you out, they might see you snap at your kid. Whatever it is that we're afraid of other moms judging us for if they could truly SEE us.

So when I asked other moms if they would ever judge another mom for asking for help, I was actually surprised that 100% said no. They either wished they could ask for help/ did ask or would never judge another mom who did. Now I realize that maybe no one would willingly admit to me that they judged another mom. But so many moms took time out of their day to make it a point to tell me they would never judge someone.

One time I was out with both of my kids and Molly wanted to push Ander in the stroller. She was not very good at it and was continually pushing the stroller into the wall. I told her she could push the stroller but I needed my hands on it to guide it. She went into a full meltdown and was screaming and crying. I told her there was no way I was letting her push the stroller alone. She could help me or walk by herself. I thought I was alone in this particular hallway, and if I'd known someone was walking behind me, I would have been mortified at her behavior, because they would see that I have not properly trained my kid and judge me. From behind me came a woman who smiled at me and said, "Good job, mom; you are being so consistent!" She didn't judge me. She remembered what it was like and encouraged me. It made my whole day. It took her one second of breath and nothing else, but it made my whole day sunny and bright.

Though we do get the highlight reel on Instagram, that is not real life. And we know that. But we do it too. We are proud of these little people we made and are raising. And when they do something right, you burst with pride and you want to tell the world. I get it. I just wish I looked at my social media through that lens. I wish I remembered there was a whole journey and blooper reel behind the highlight reel.

I wrote this book to show YOU the journey, complete with bloopers. I hope you can relate to parts of my story in some small way. And feel like you are not alone. Because I let myself feel alone. But I know I wasn't.

I don't hope to gain anything from this book. I don't think it'll make a ton of money or bring me fame. I don't want to start a podcast or blog. Although - let's think big here for a minute - maybe one day this book will find its way into the hands of a Duggar. Guys, then I would have really made it.

I think, though, apart from all of that, beyond just hoping to entertain, I knew I would be remiss if I didn't tell you about another part of my story. A part I have alluded to and touched on, but I think I need to share it with you plainly. I believe in Jesus Christ. I know He is The One who has carried me through this journey. And is carrying me through every day. I have amazing people who surround me. I have an incredible village. But that village and my people mean nothing without The Lord. He is the reason I can get up in the morning. His overwhelming love sustains me even when I am at my lowest. Friend, if you are reading this and you do not know my Jesus, I wish I could look you in the eye and tell you about Him. I know He created this Earth and He is holy and perfect. I believe with my whole heart that I could never do anything to earn His love, I have messed up countless times and I will again. I just know that many years ago God sent His son to Earth to die on a cross. He did that so I did not have to die. He died on a cross and took my place because of my sin and shortcomings; I deserved to die, but He did that for me. And in doing that, He made a way for me to be with Him and have a relationship with Him. I believe He did those things; I believe the Bible is His love letter to me, telling me how good He is and how to get to know Him. Why am I telling you this? Maybe this book took a huge left turn for you. But I have to tell you the full secret to any success I have as a mom. I have walked some lows, but I never did it alone. Even when I feel alone or get overwhelmed, He is never far away. His love for me was right by me. I really do not believe in coincidences; I believe that God is All-Knowing and He can turn anything that happens in this life into good. I don't mean I think that He makes bad things happen. No way. But I think we make choices that lead to things that can be hard, and in His great love for us, He can make beauty from our broken lives. I know that because I have lived it. You've read my story; you've seen it all.

People have said to me they don't know how I labored for so long. Or had a VBAC. I did not do those things on my own; I had a secret. I don't want Him to be a secret. I want to tell you and everyone I know that He saved me and is walking with me every day, helping me.

John 16:23
'These things I have spoken to you, that in Me you may have peace. In the world you will have tribulation; but be of good cheer, I have overcome the world."

Made in the USA
Monee, IL
10 May 2020